INTERIOR DESIGN
COLORING BOOK

UNLEASH YOUR CREATIVITY AND DIVE INTO
40 BEAUTIFUL CREATED ROOM DESIGNS.

Markus Mangold

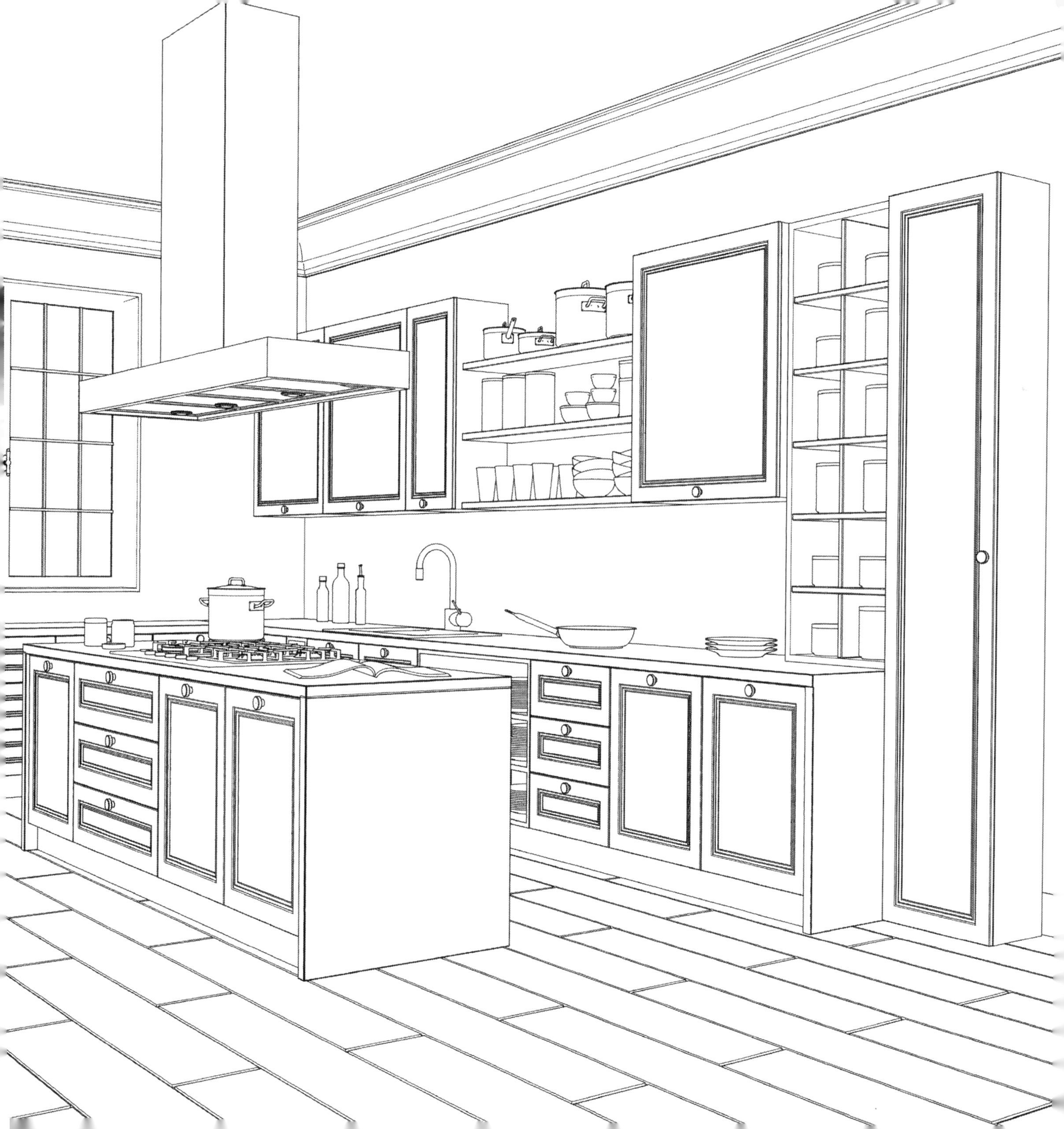

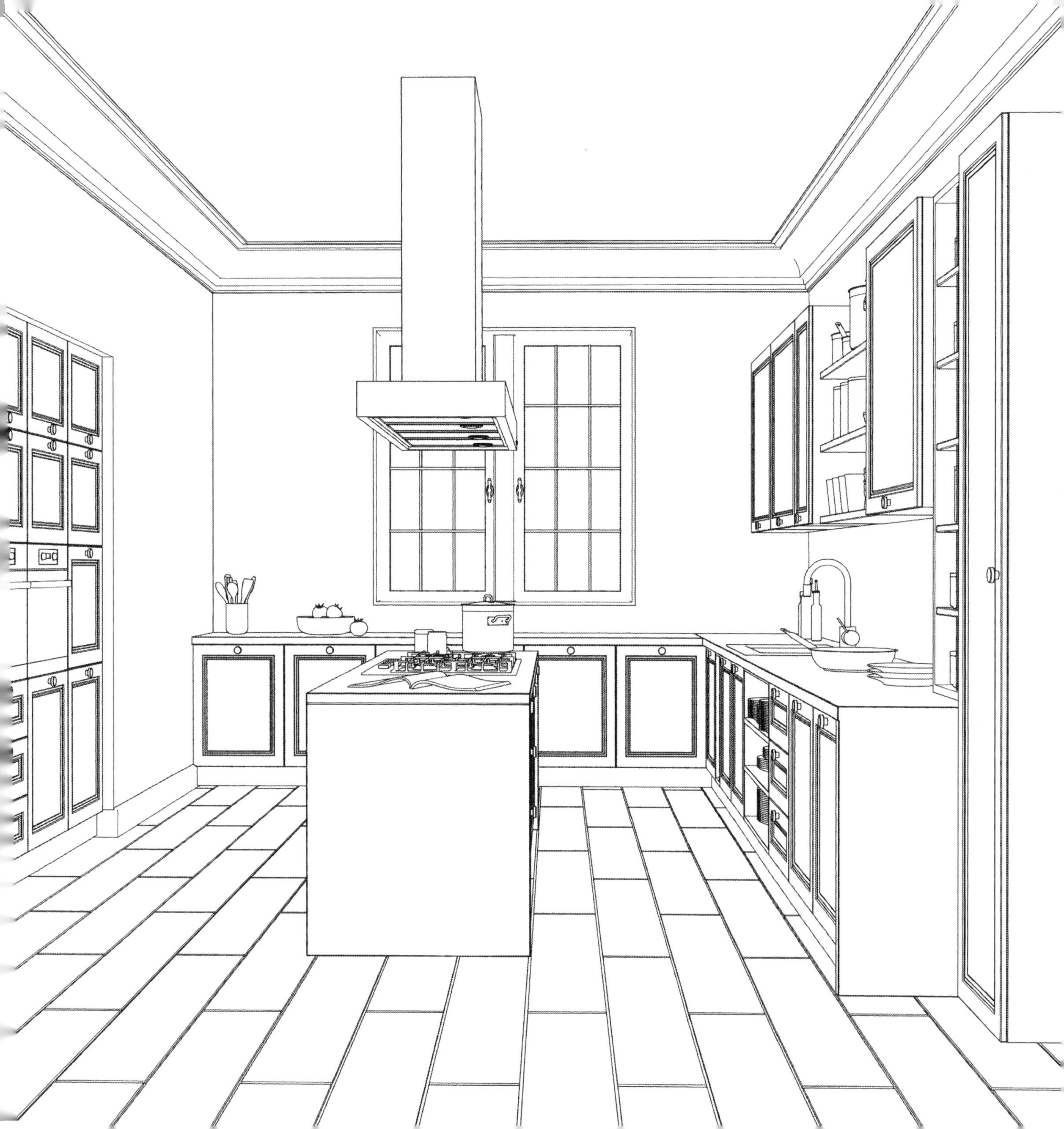

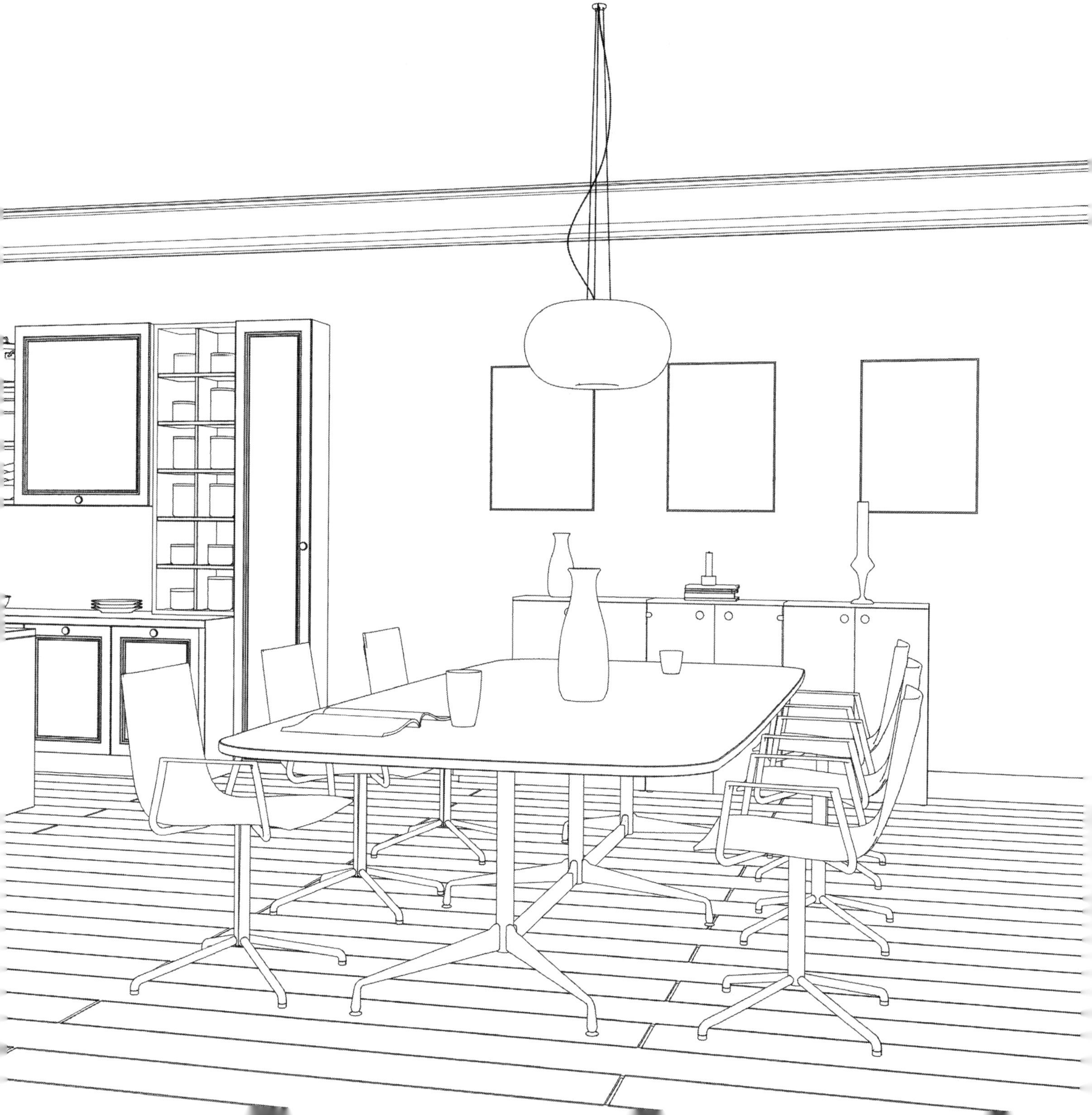

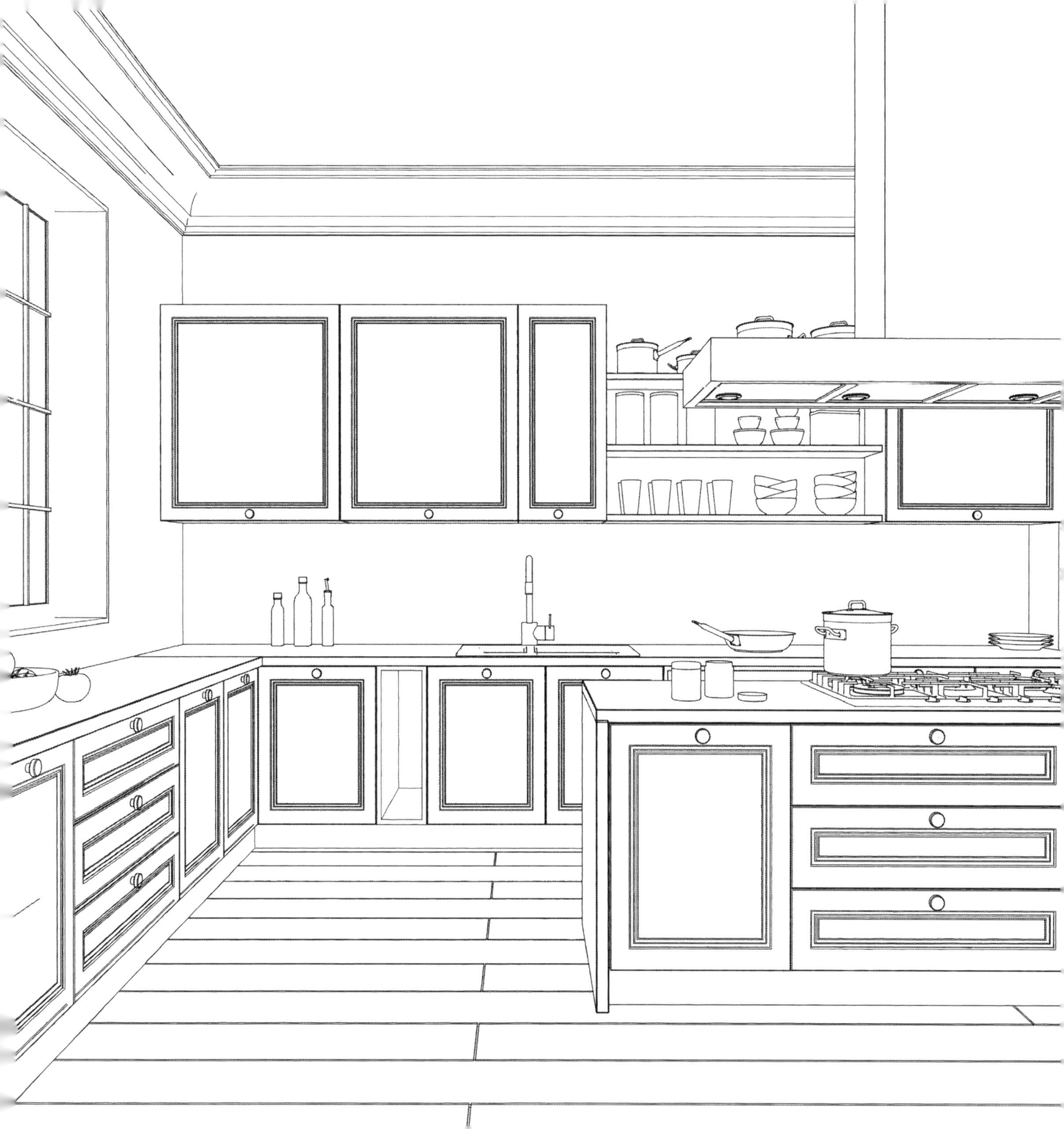

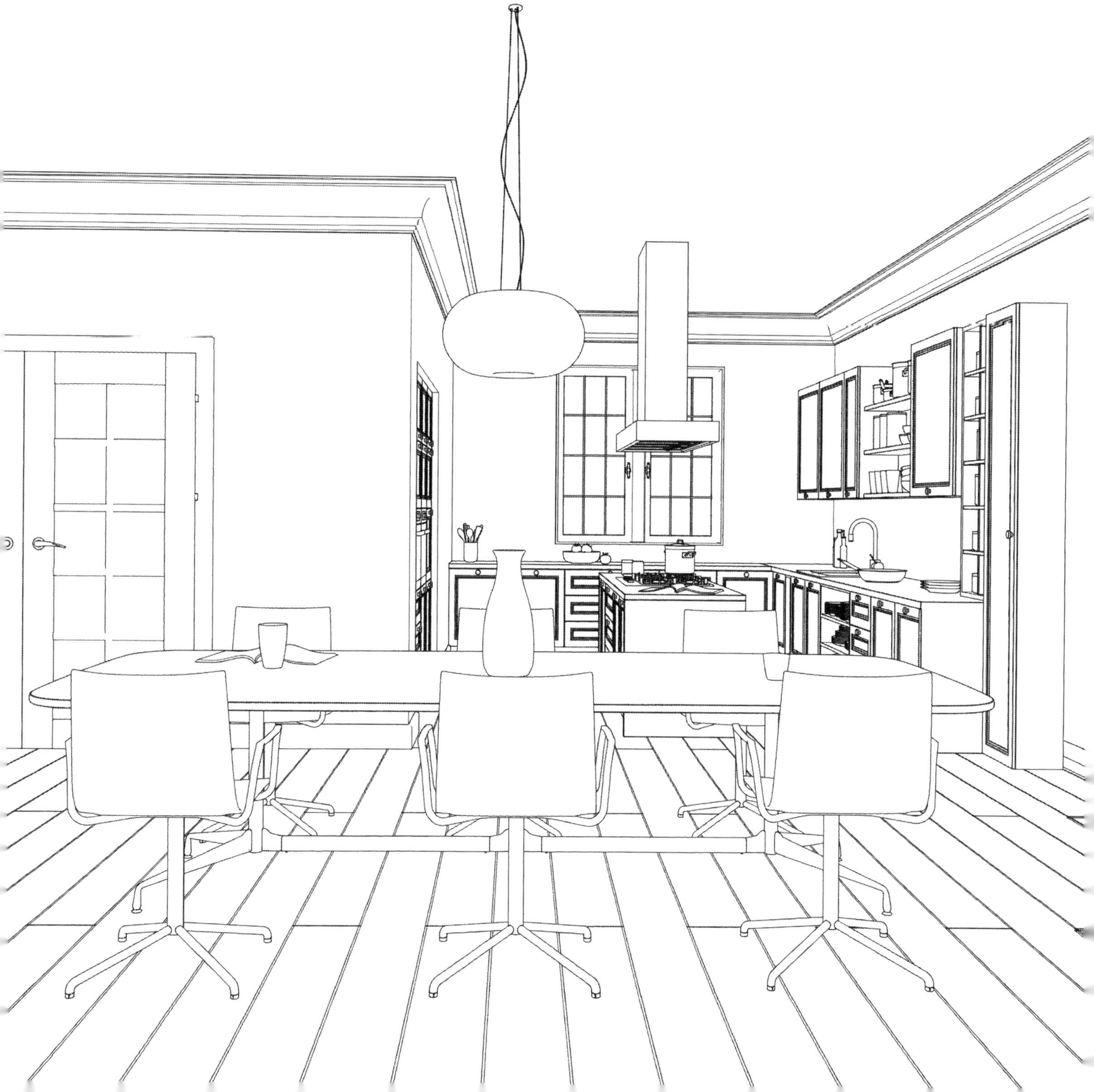

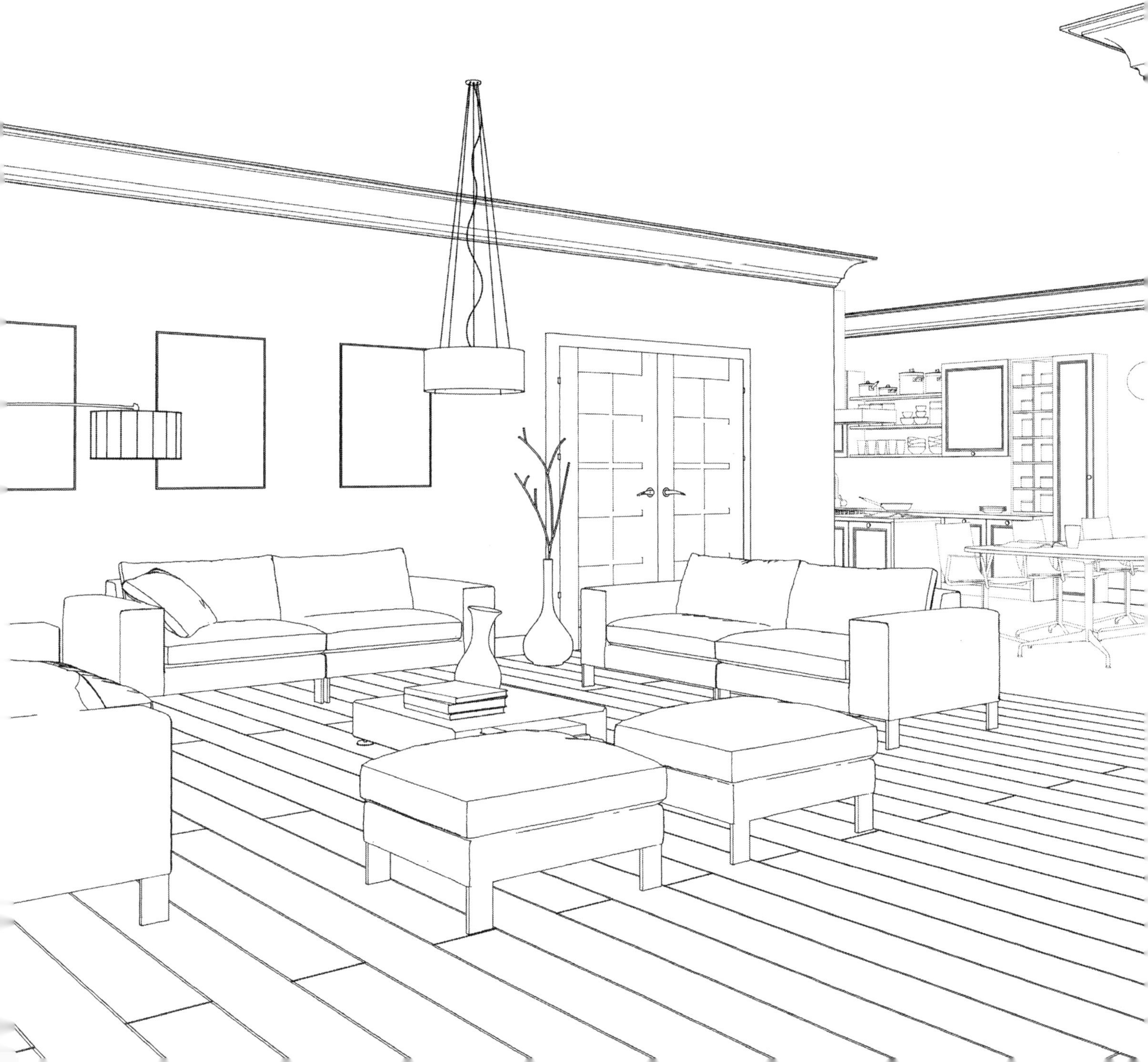

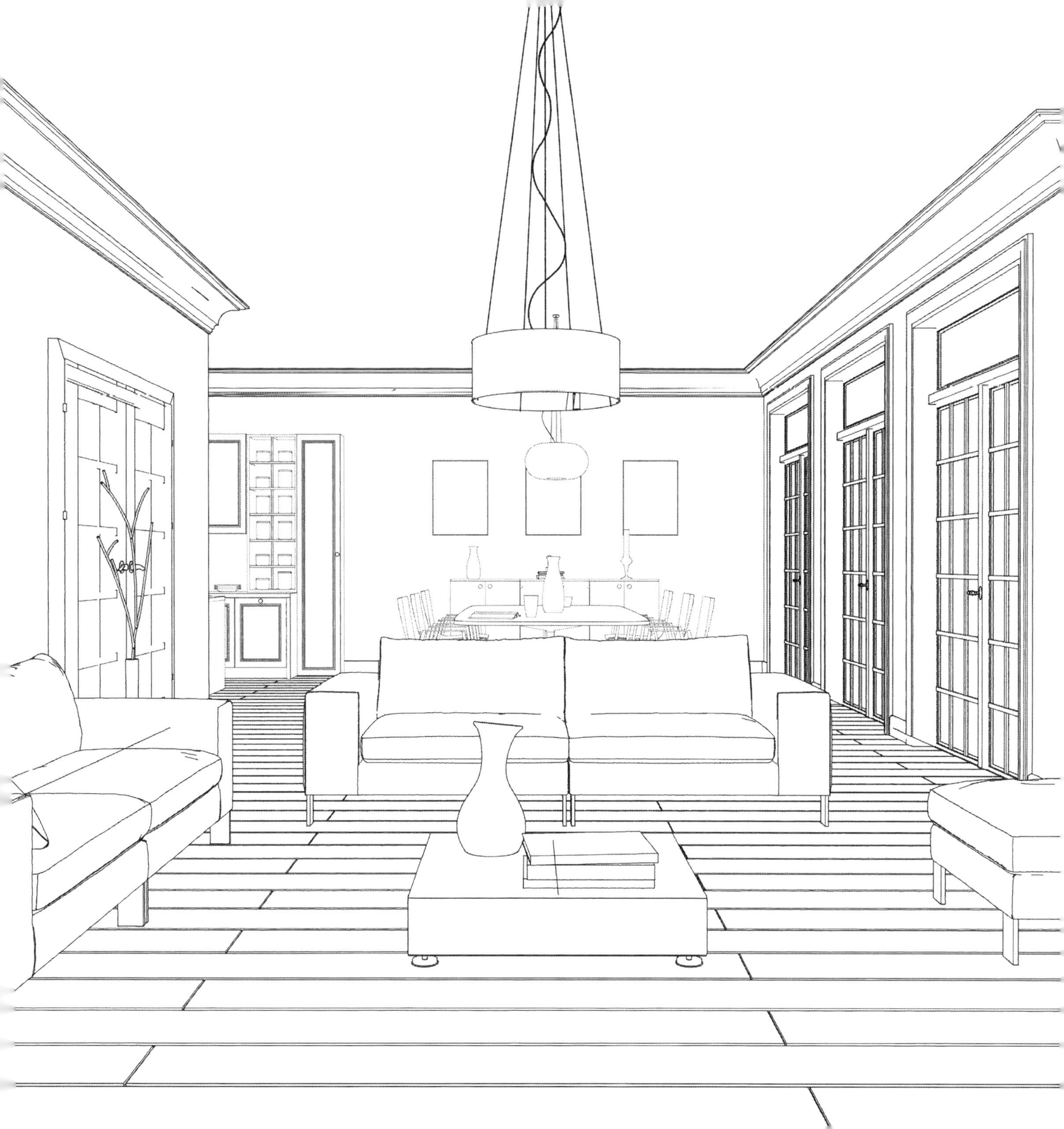

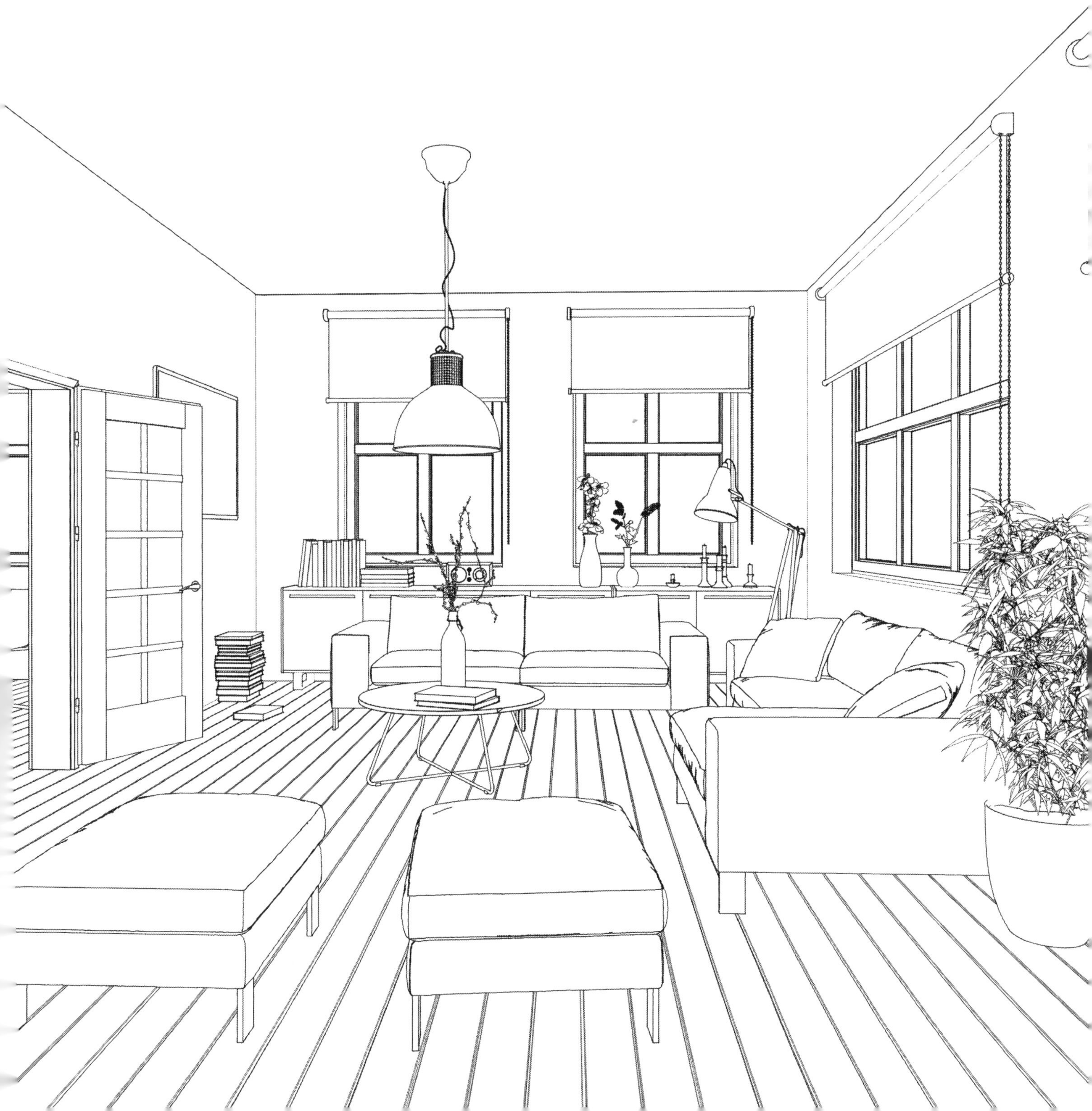

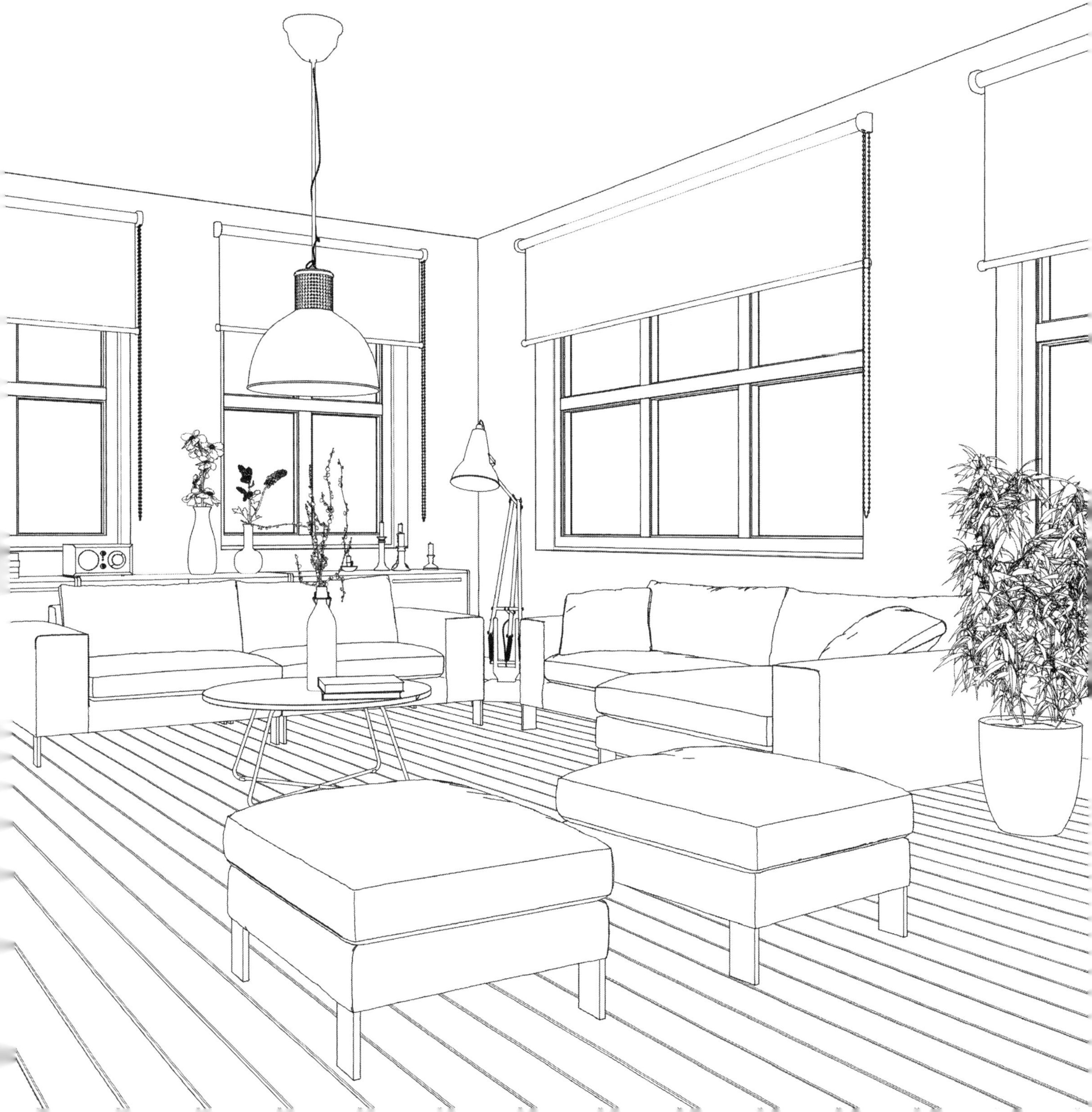

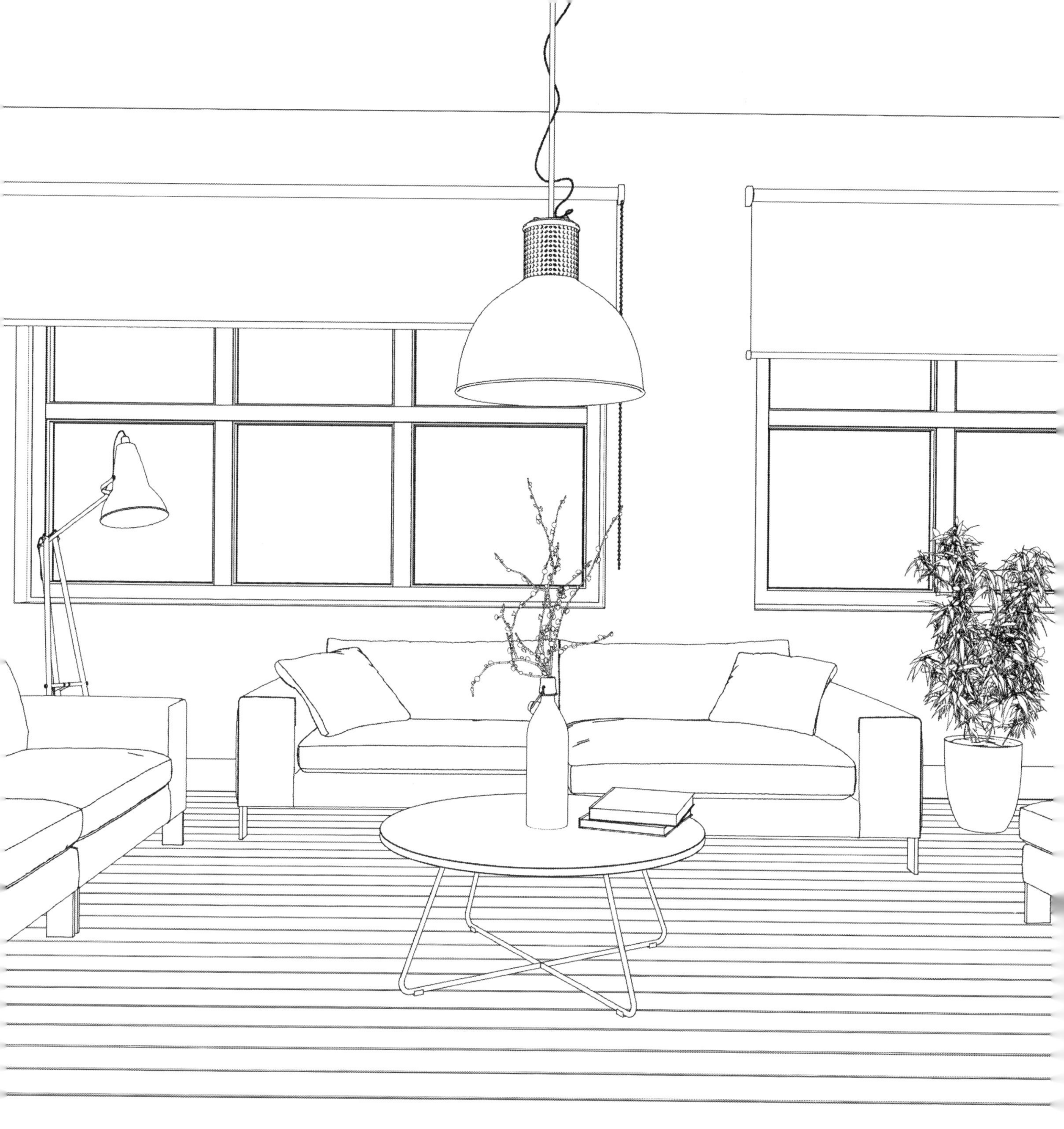

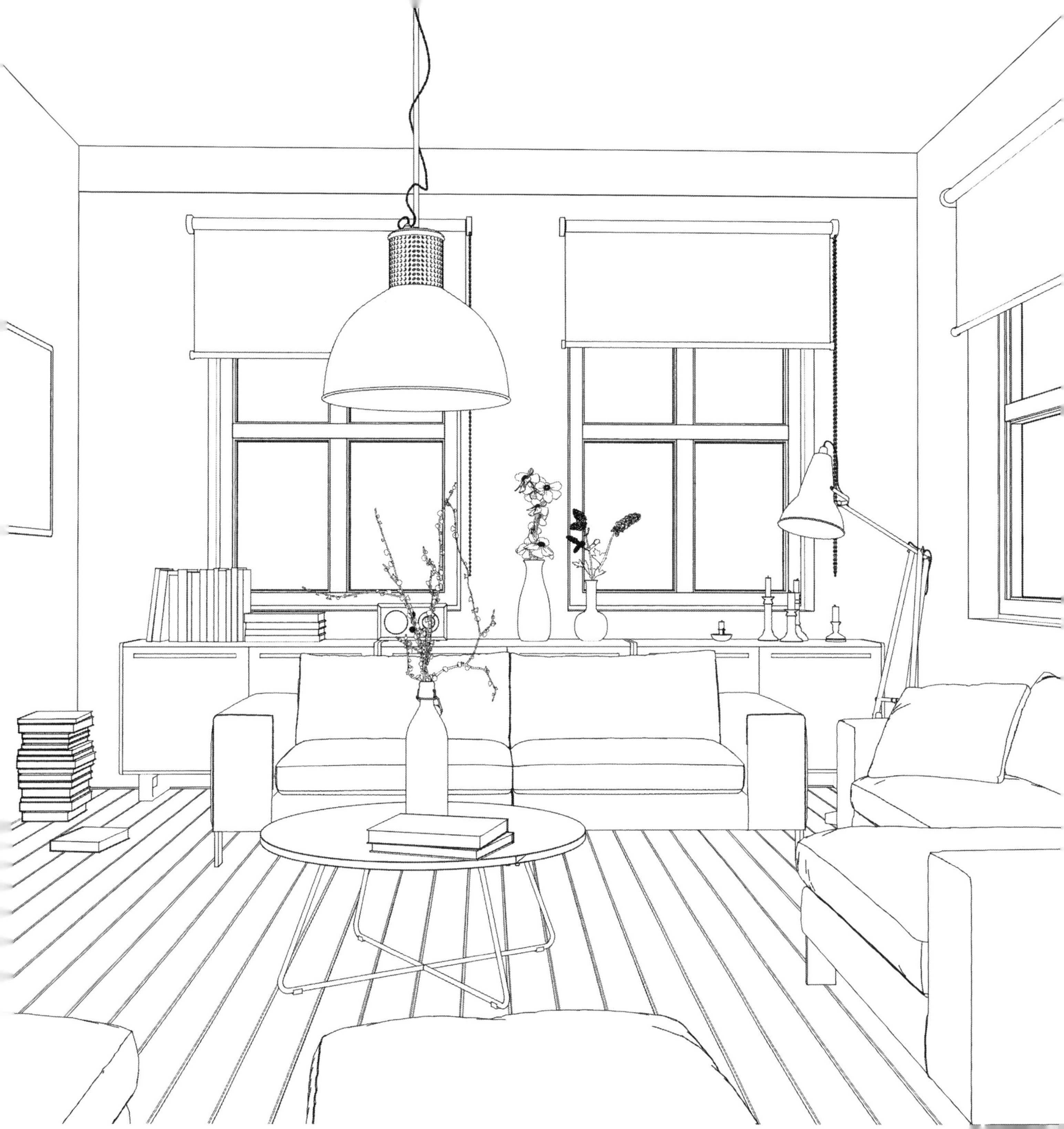

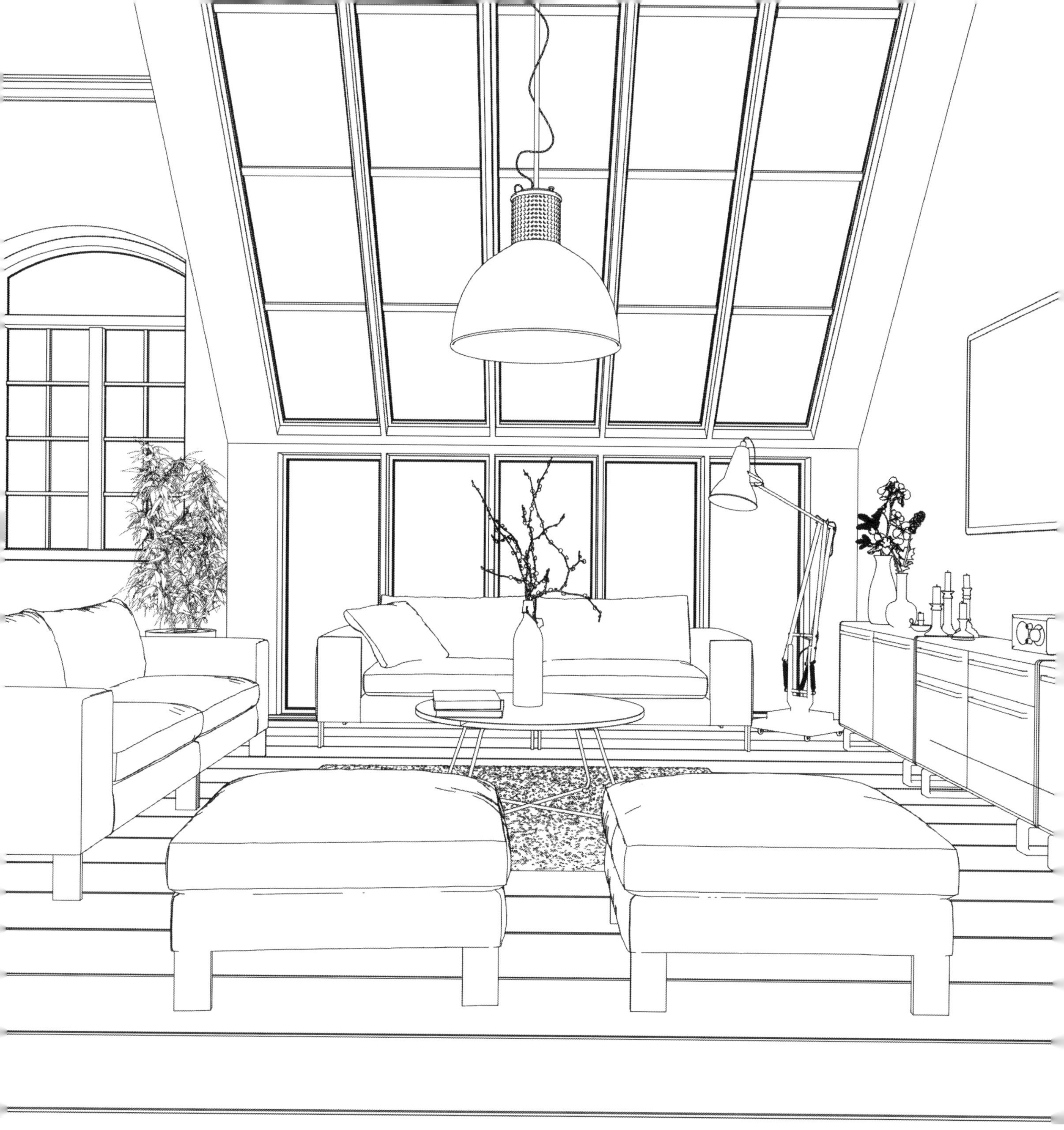

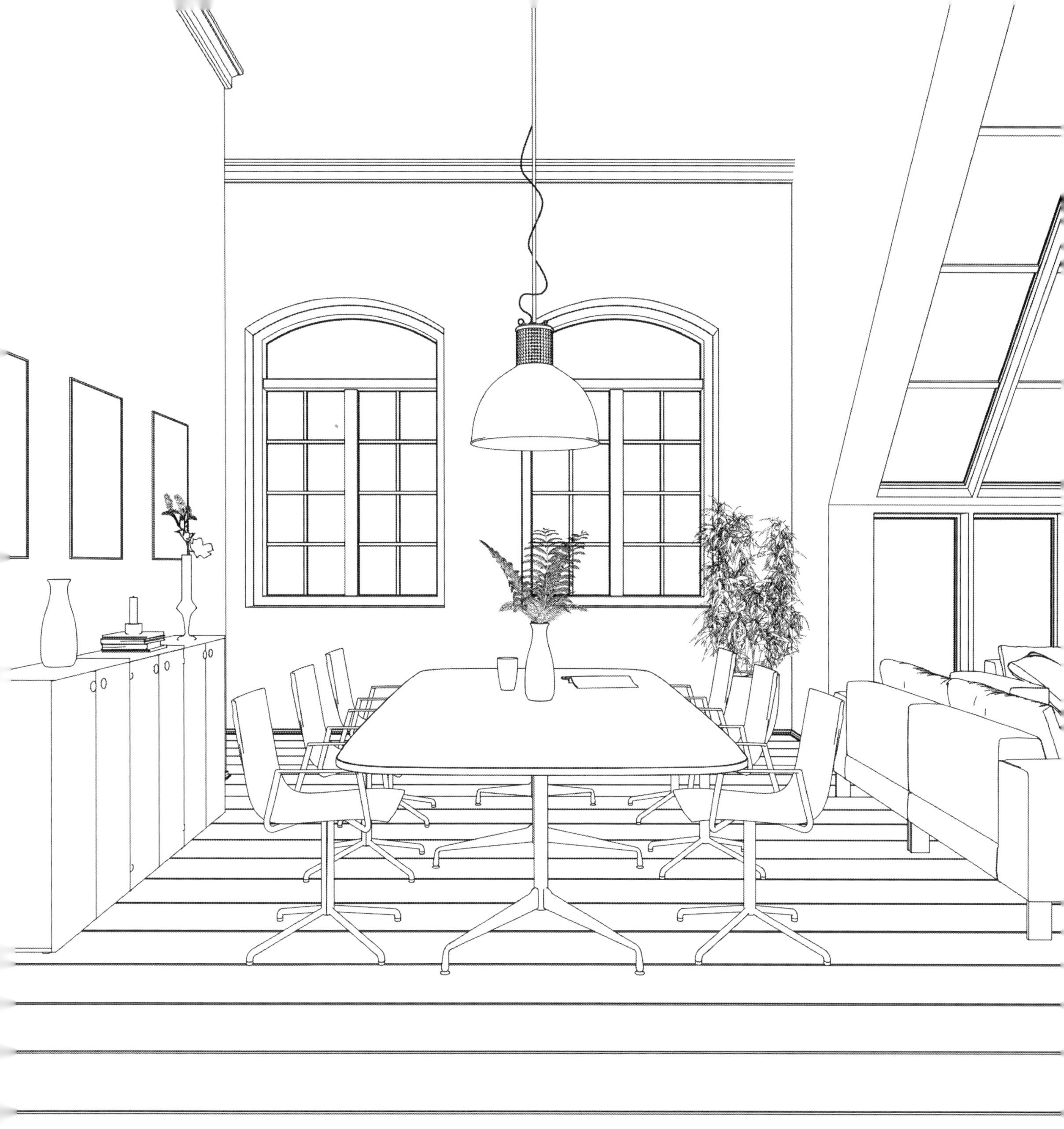

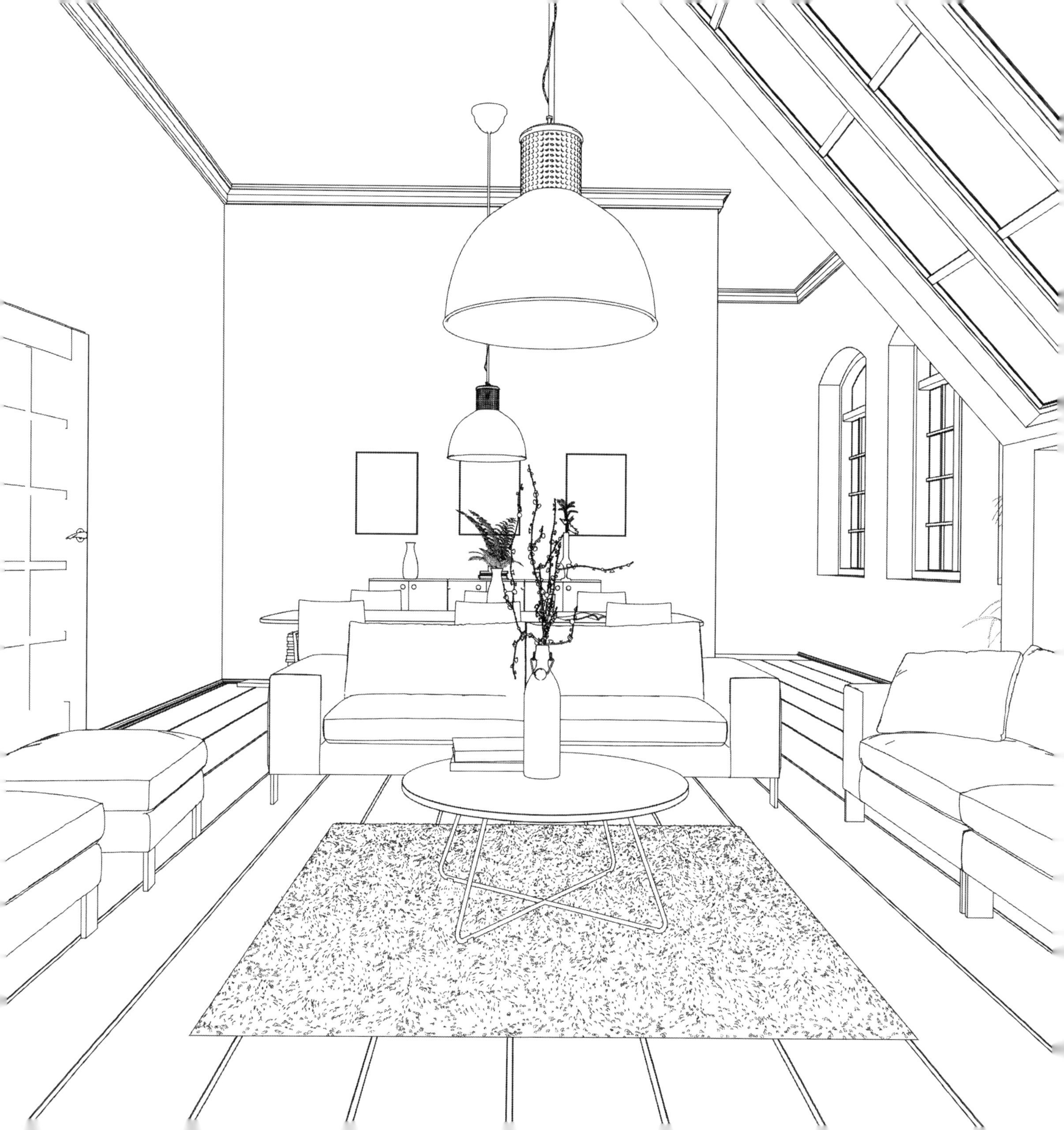

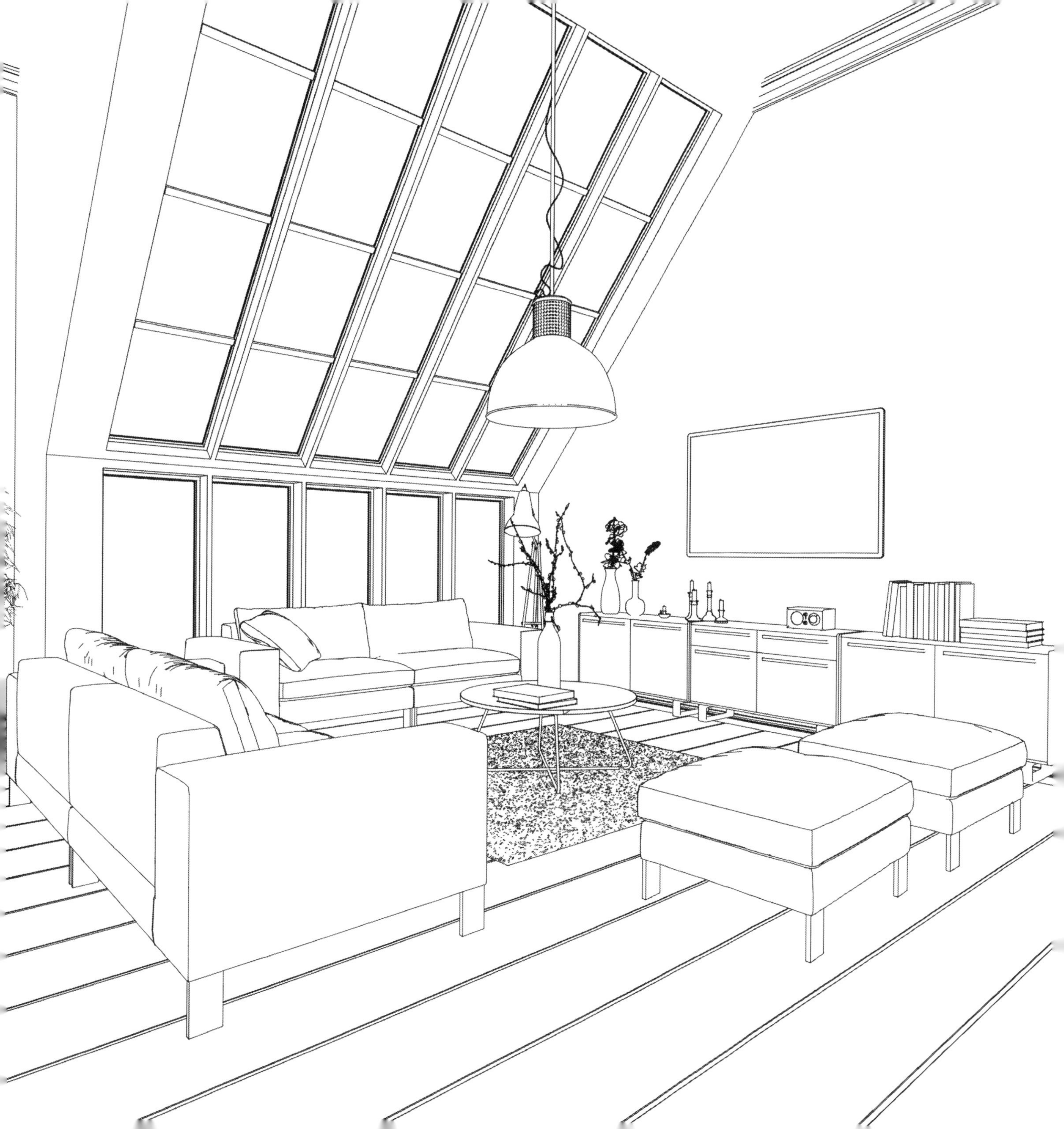

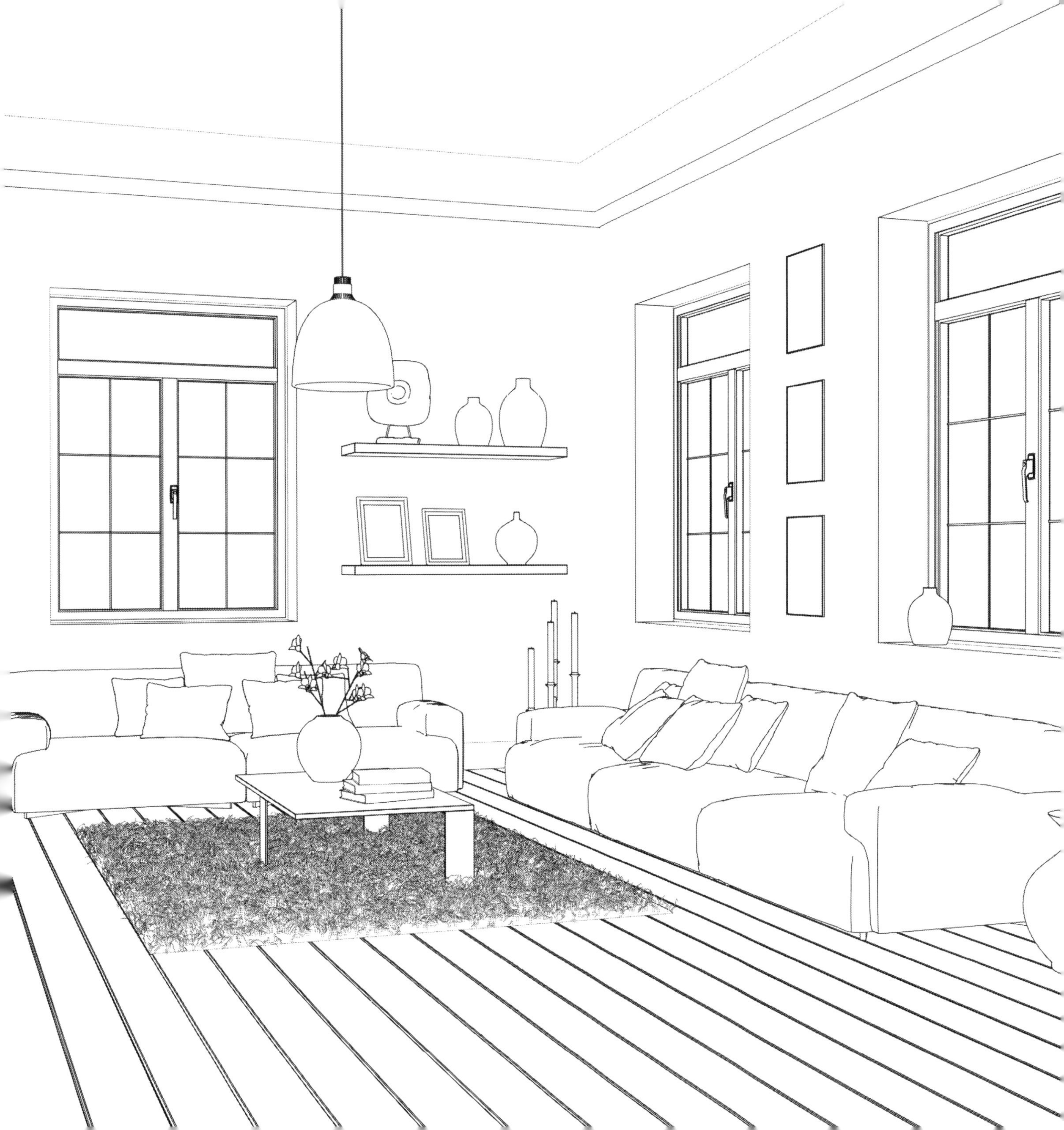

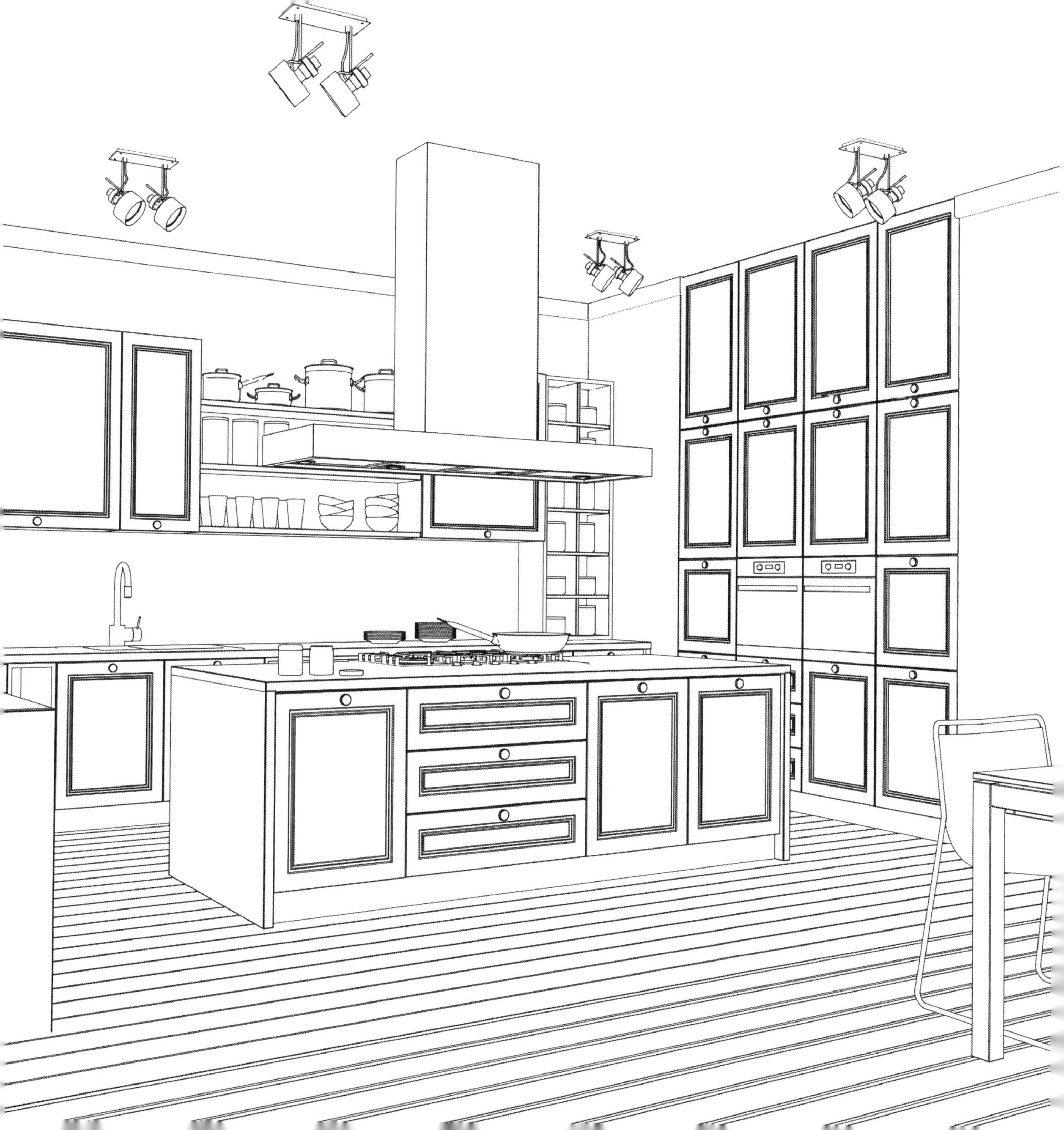

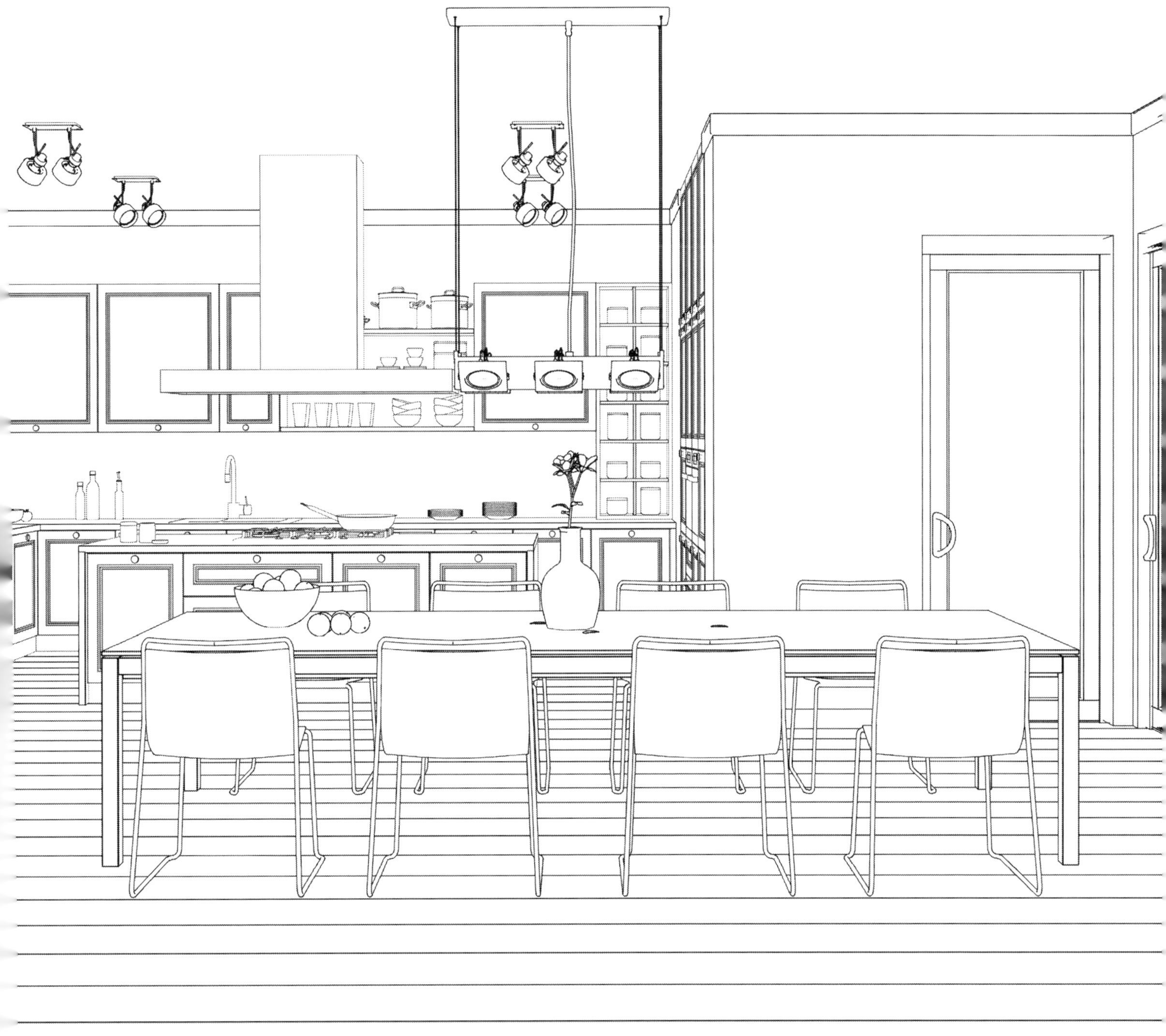

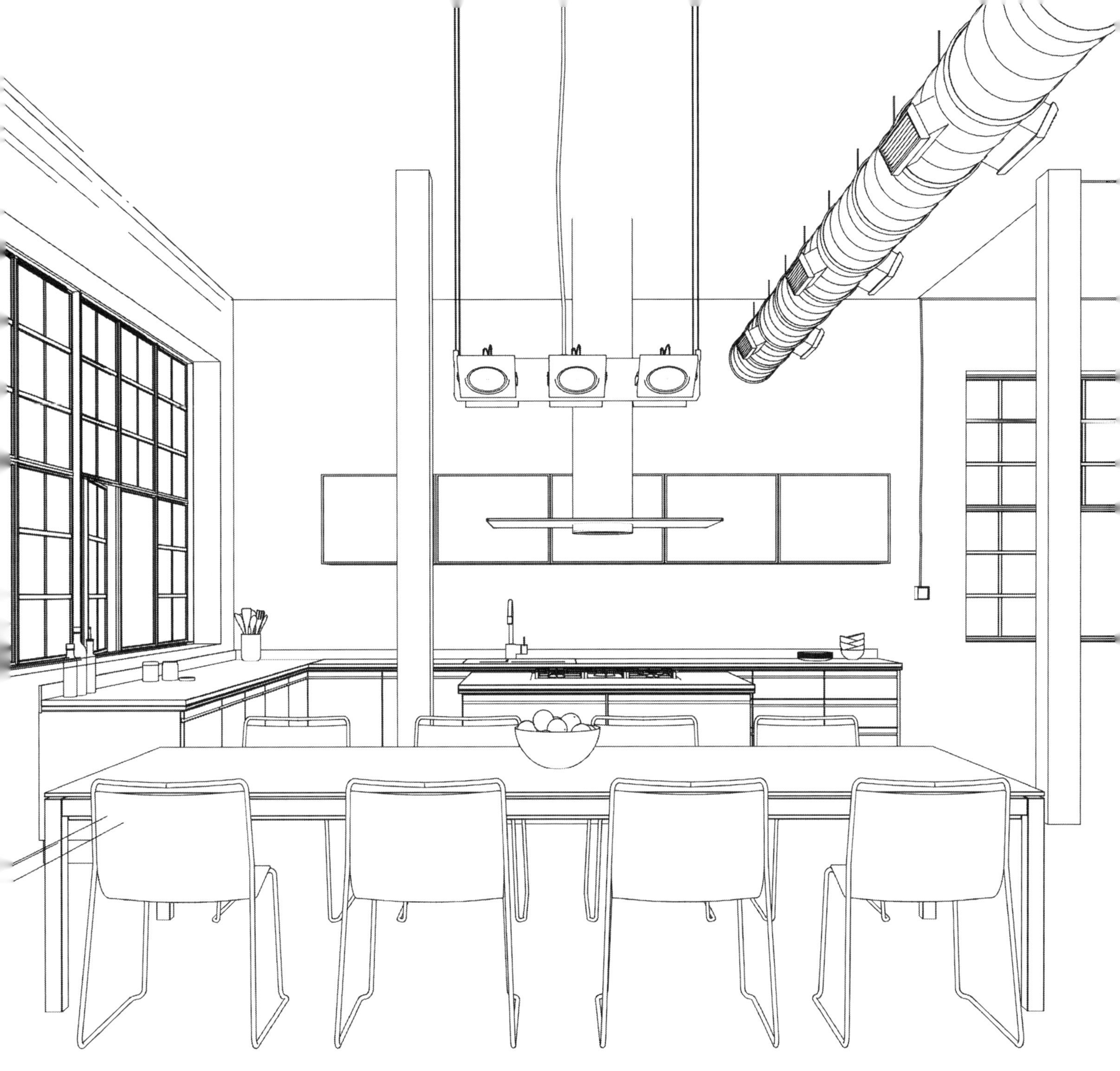

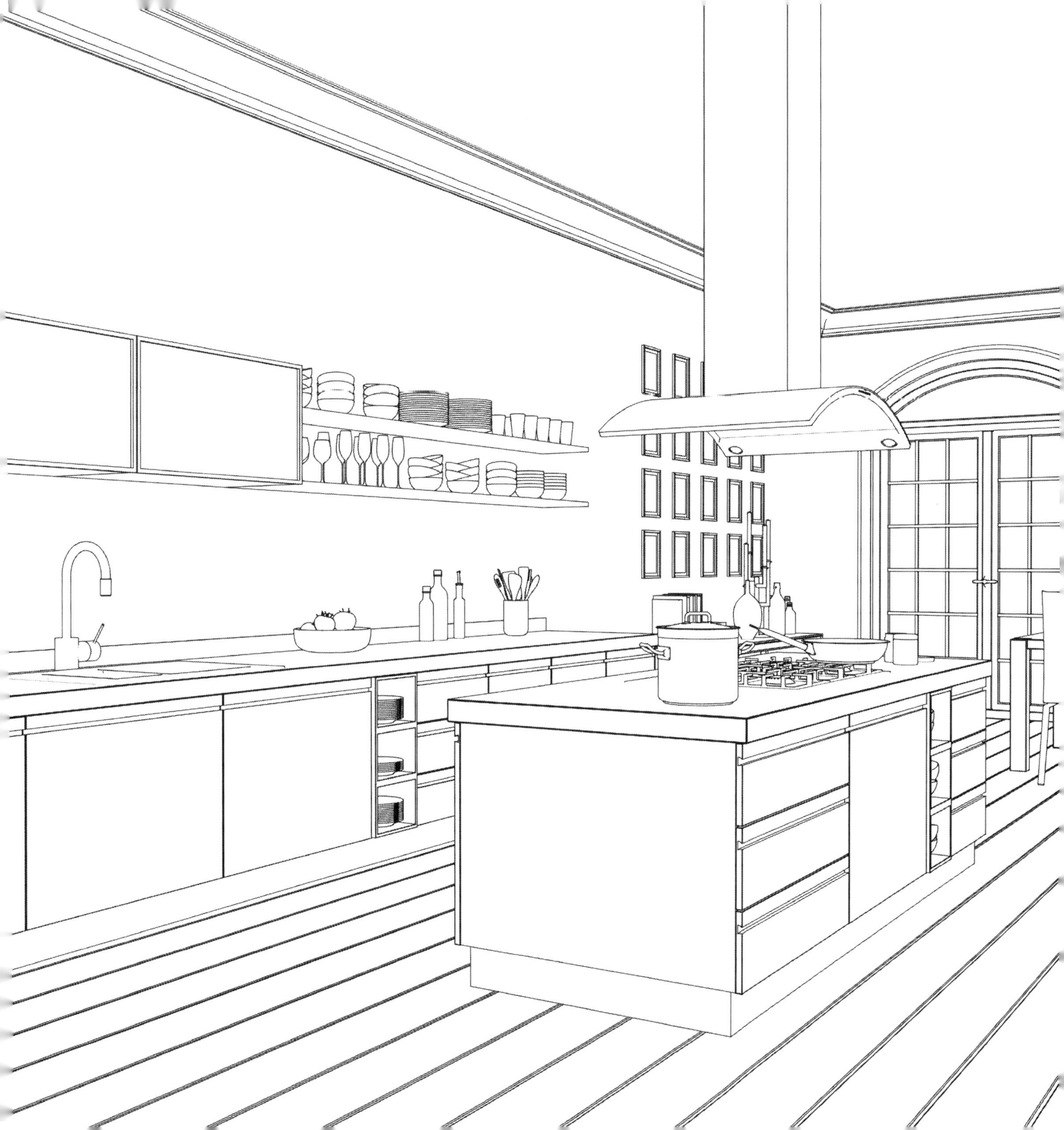

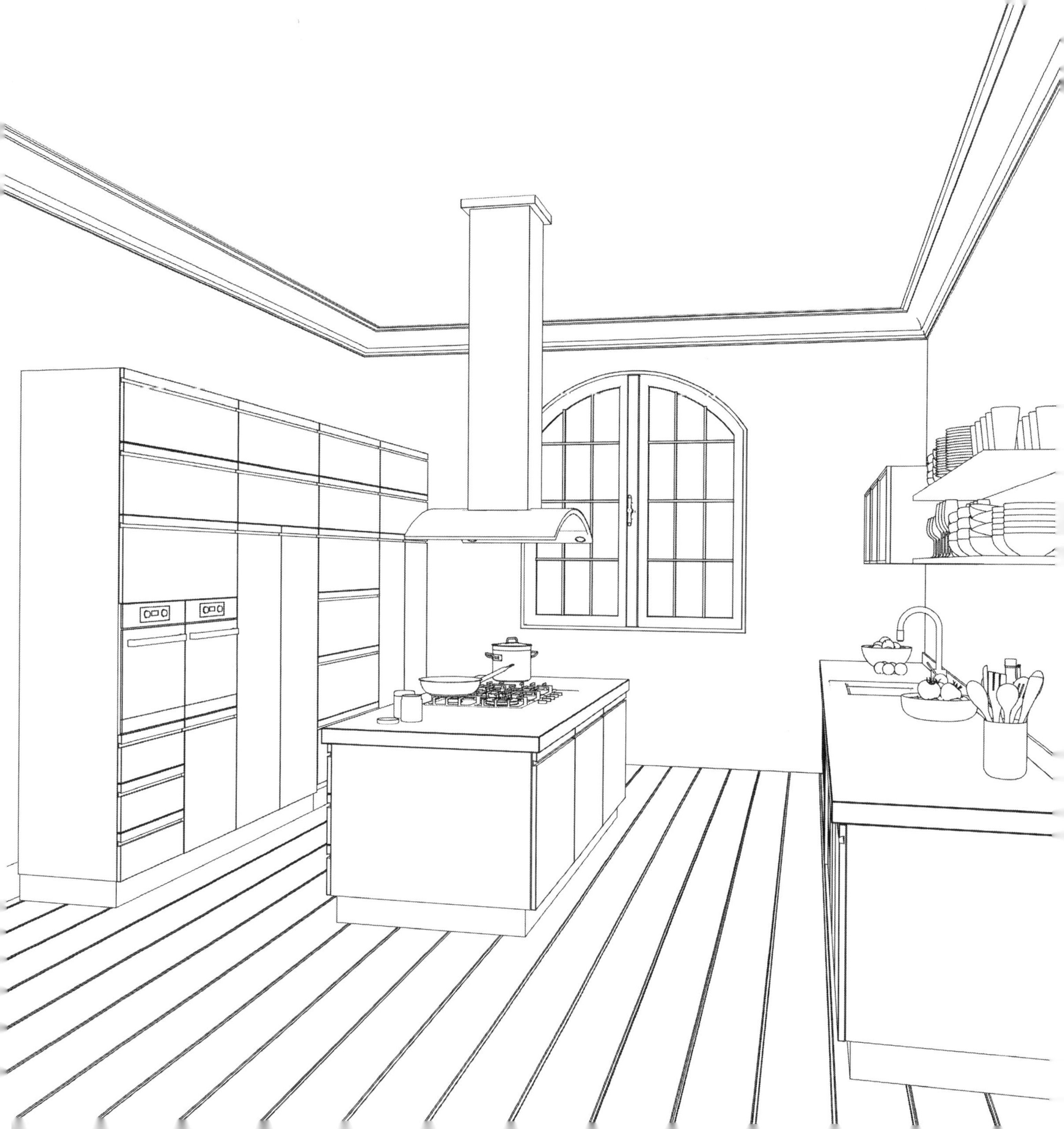

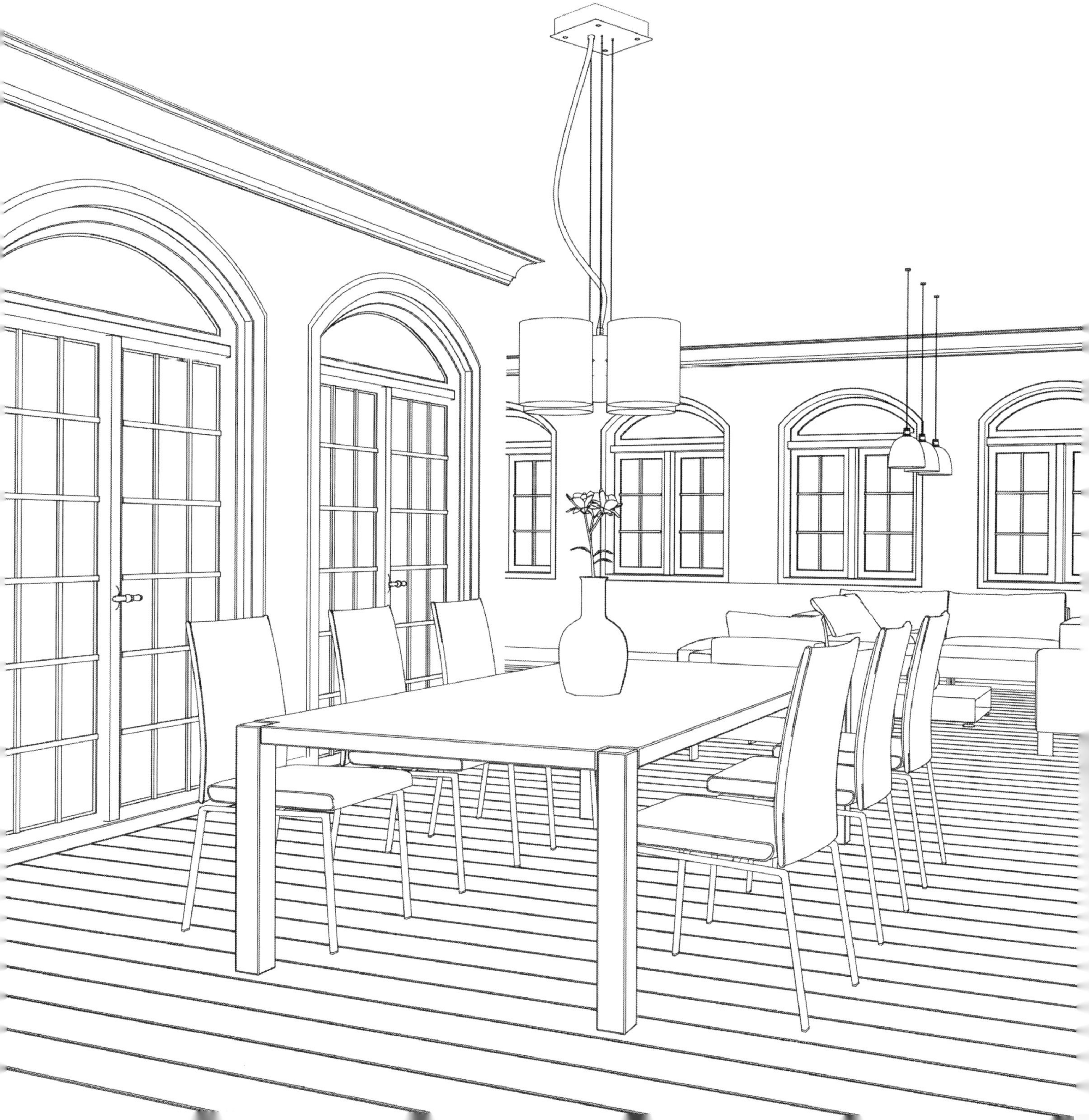

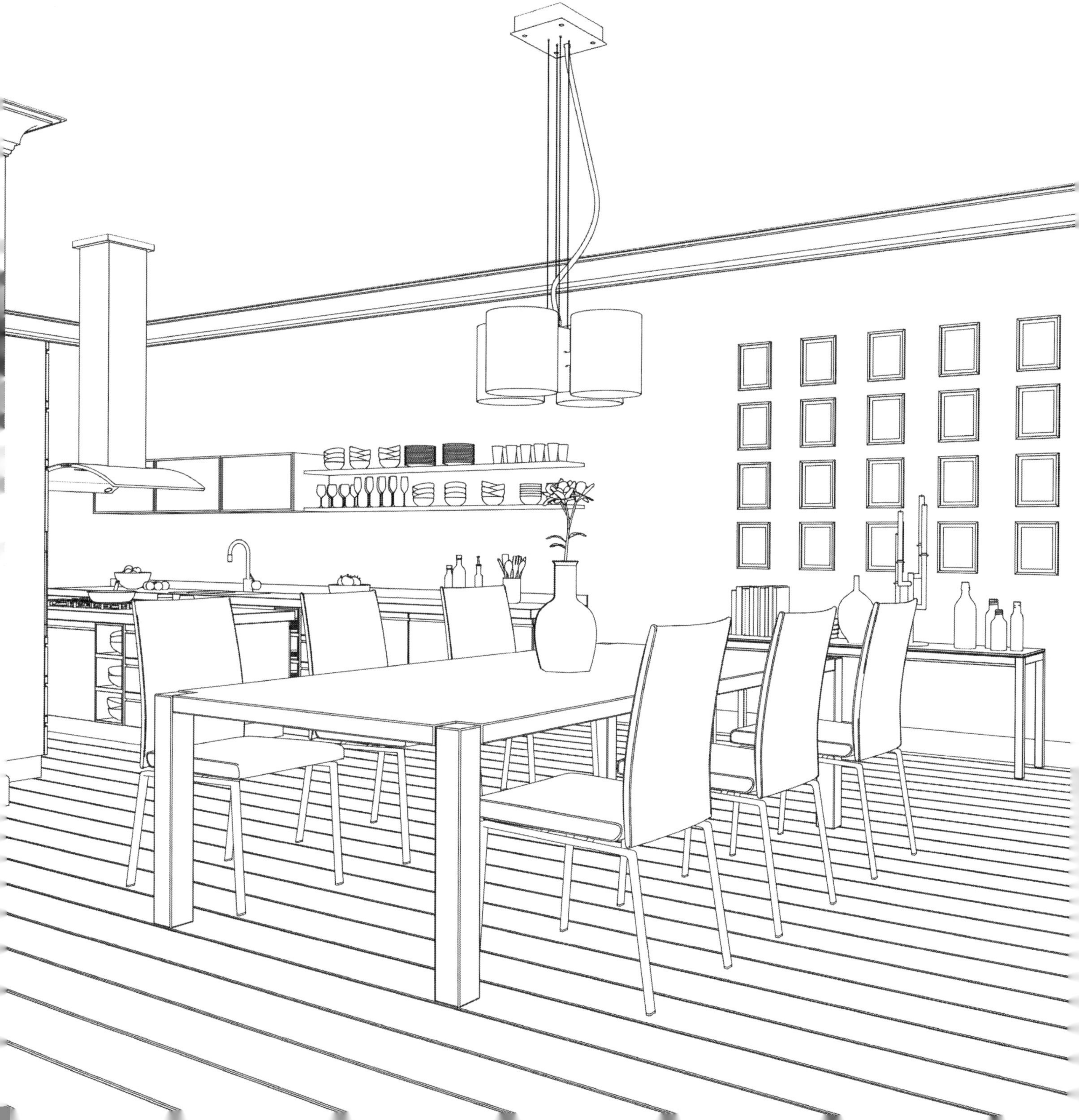

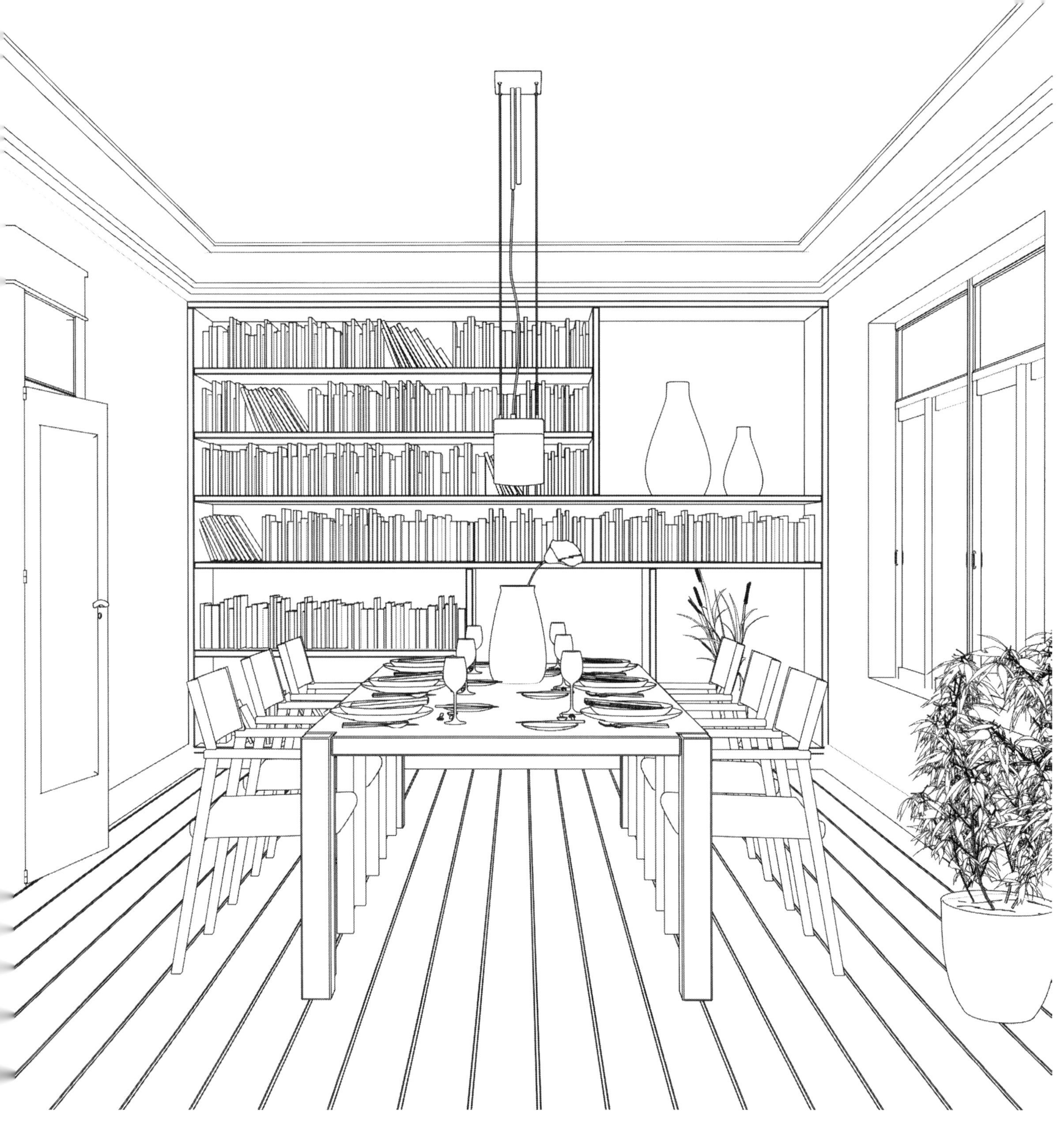

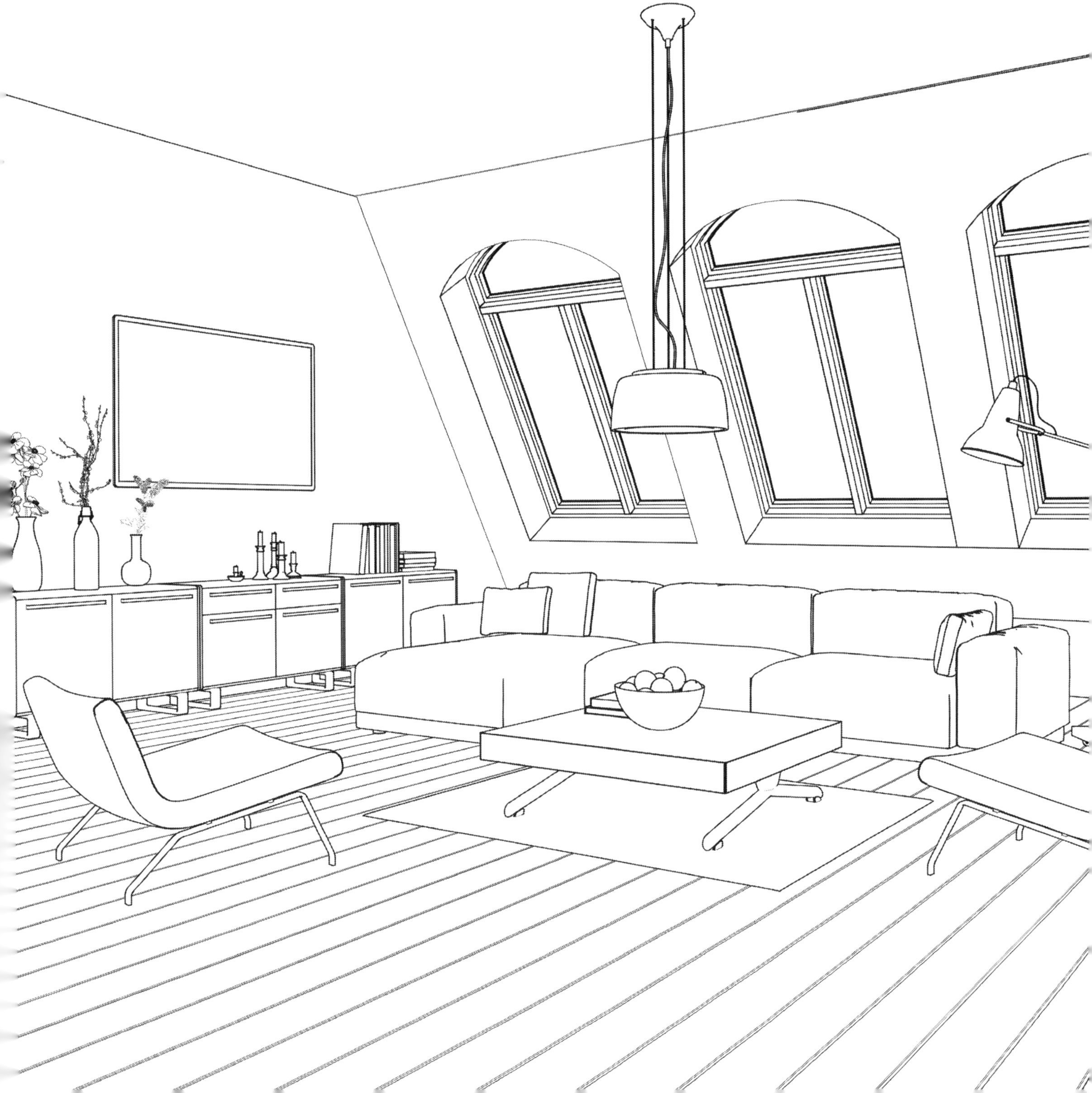

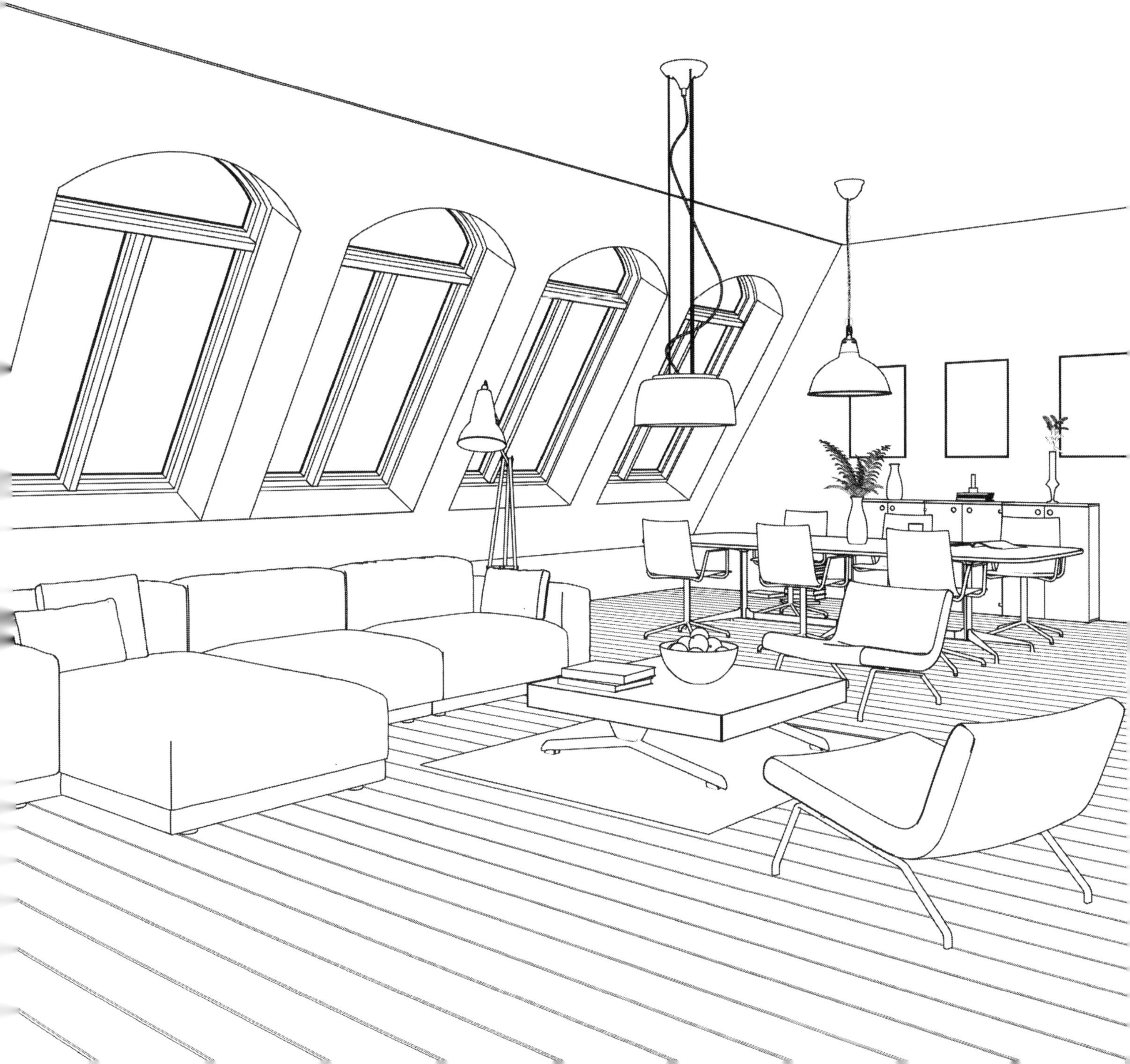

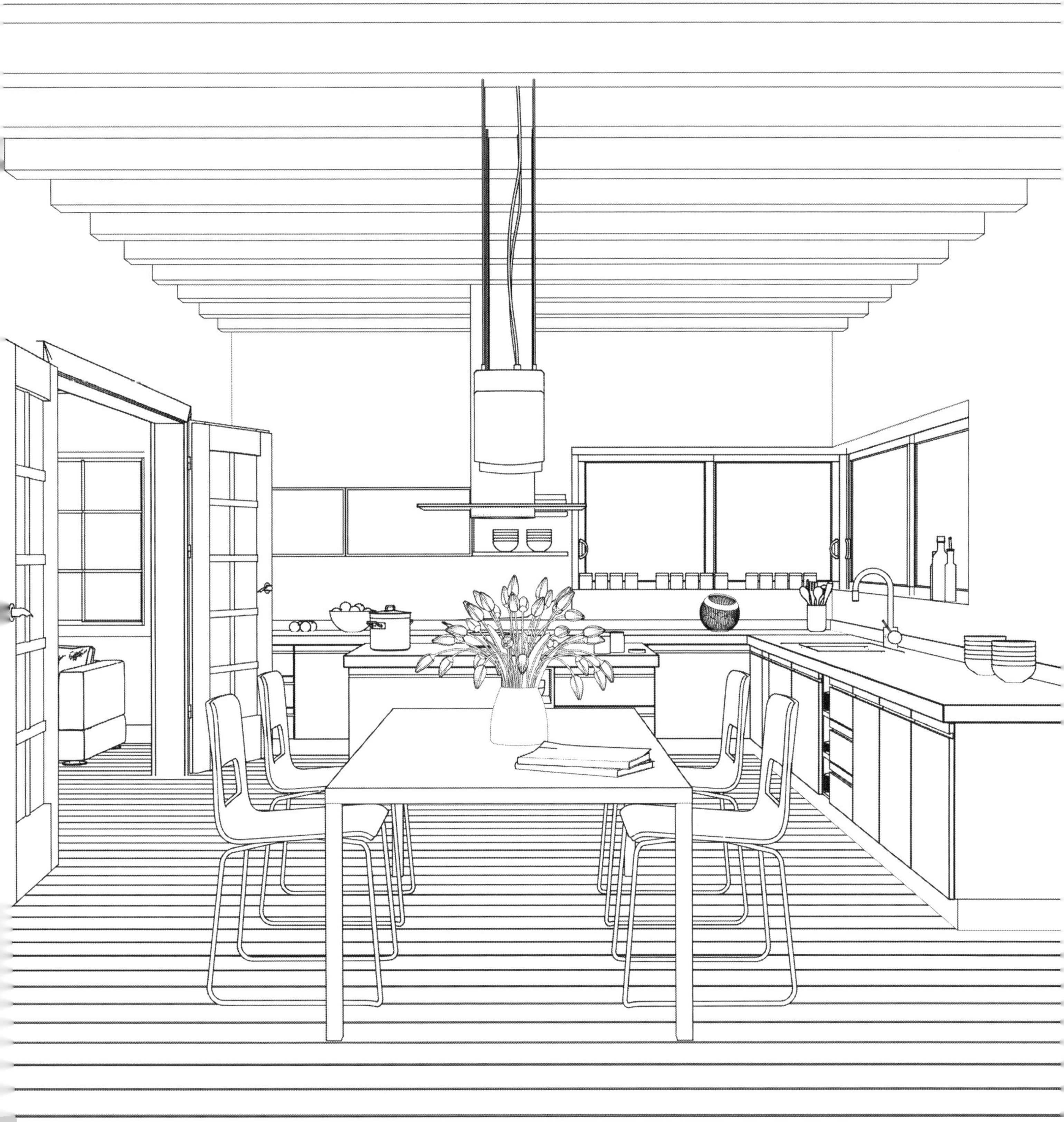

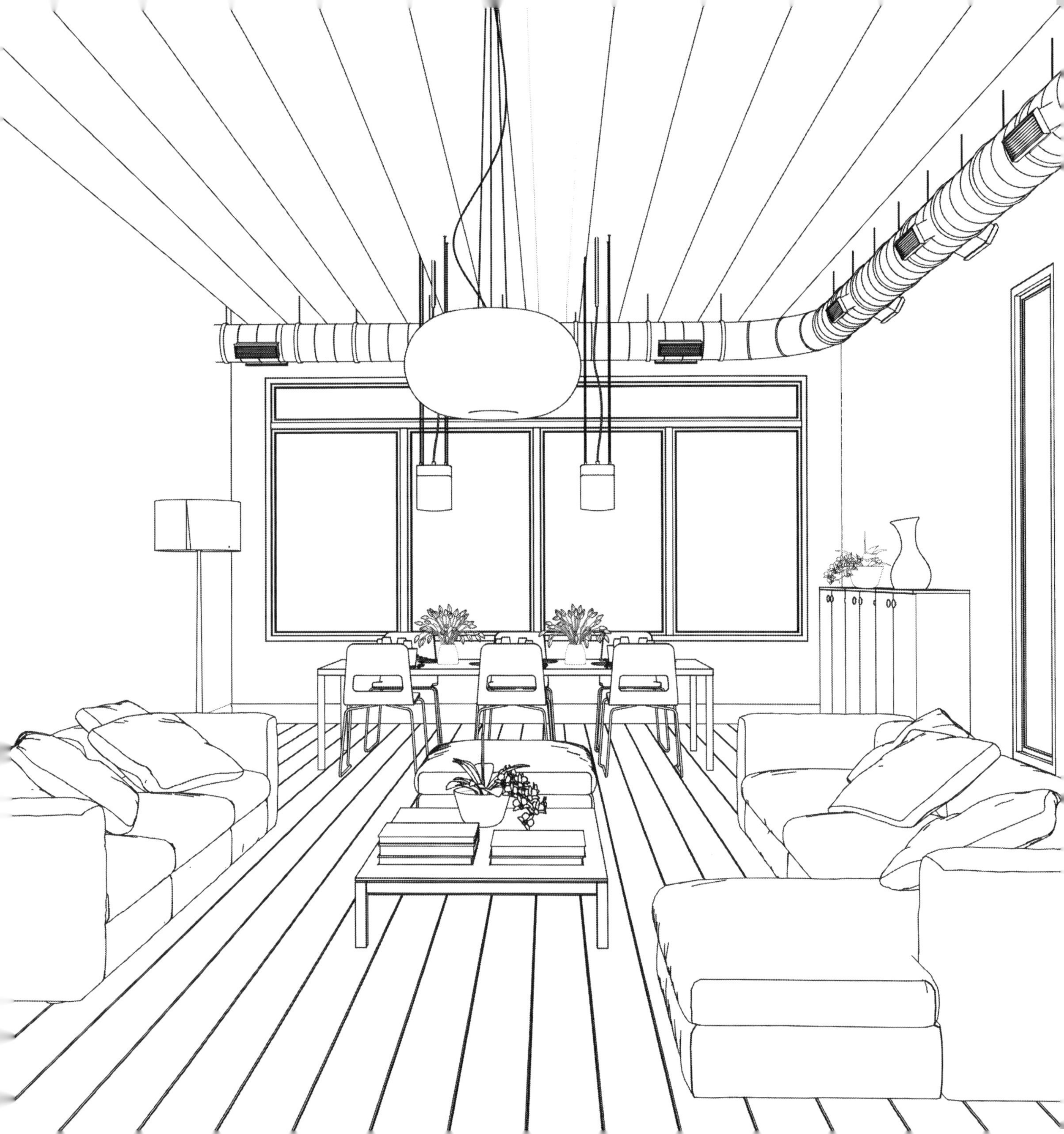

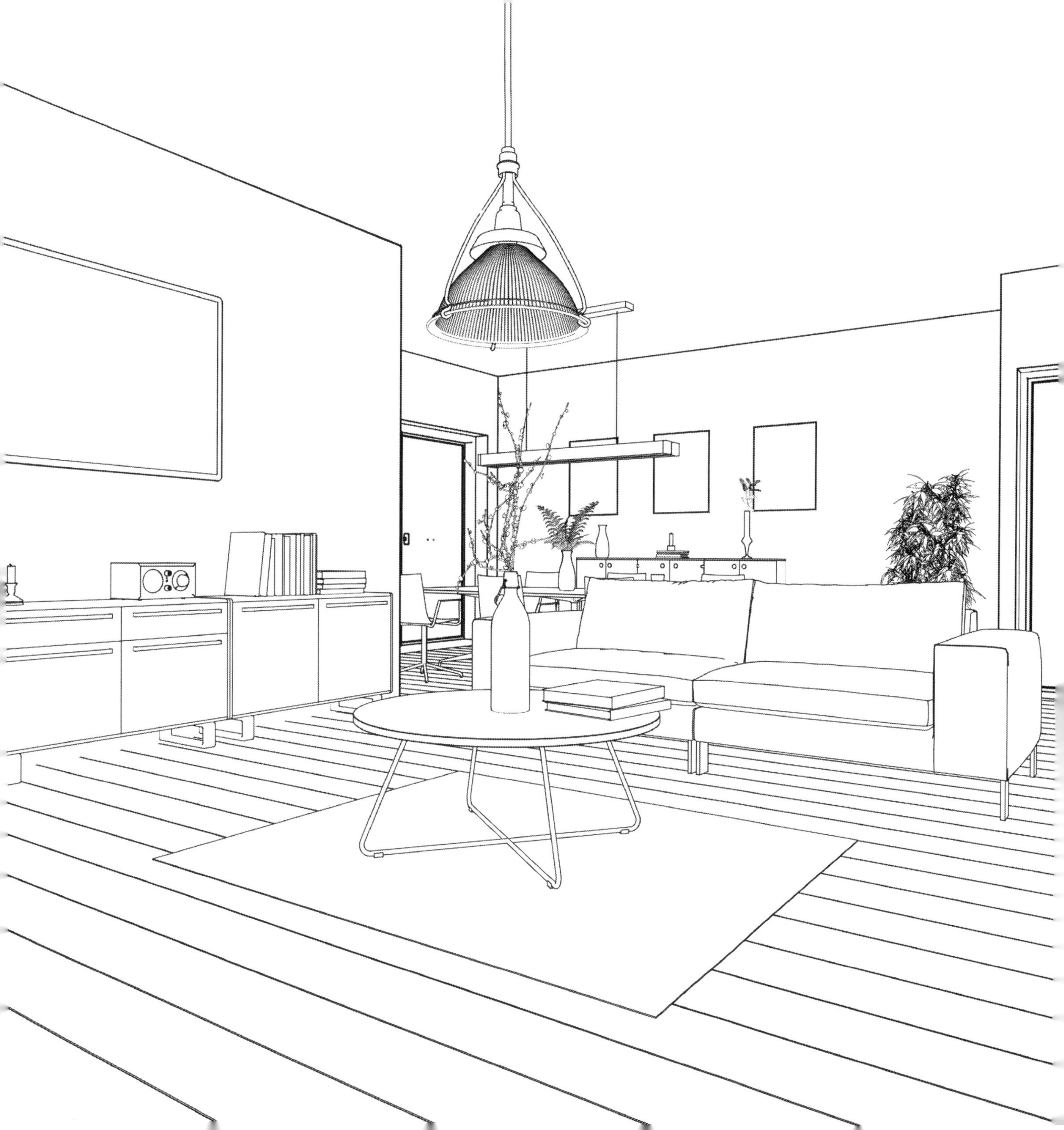

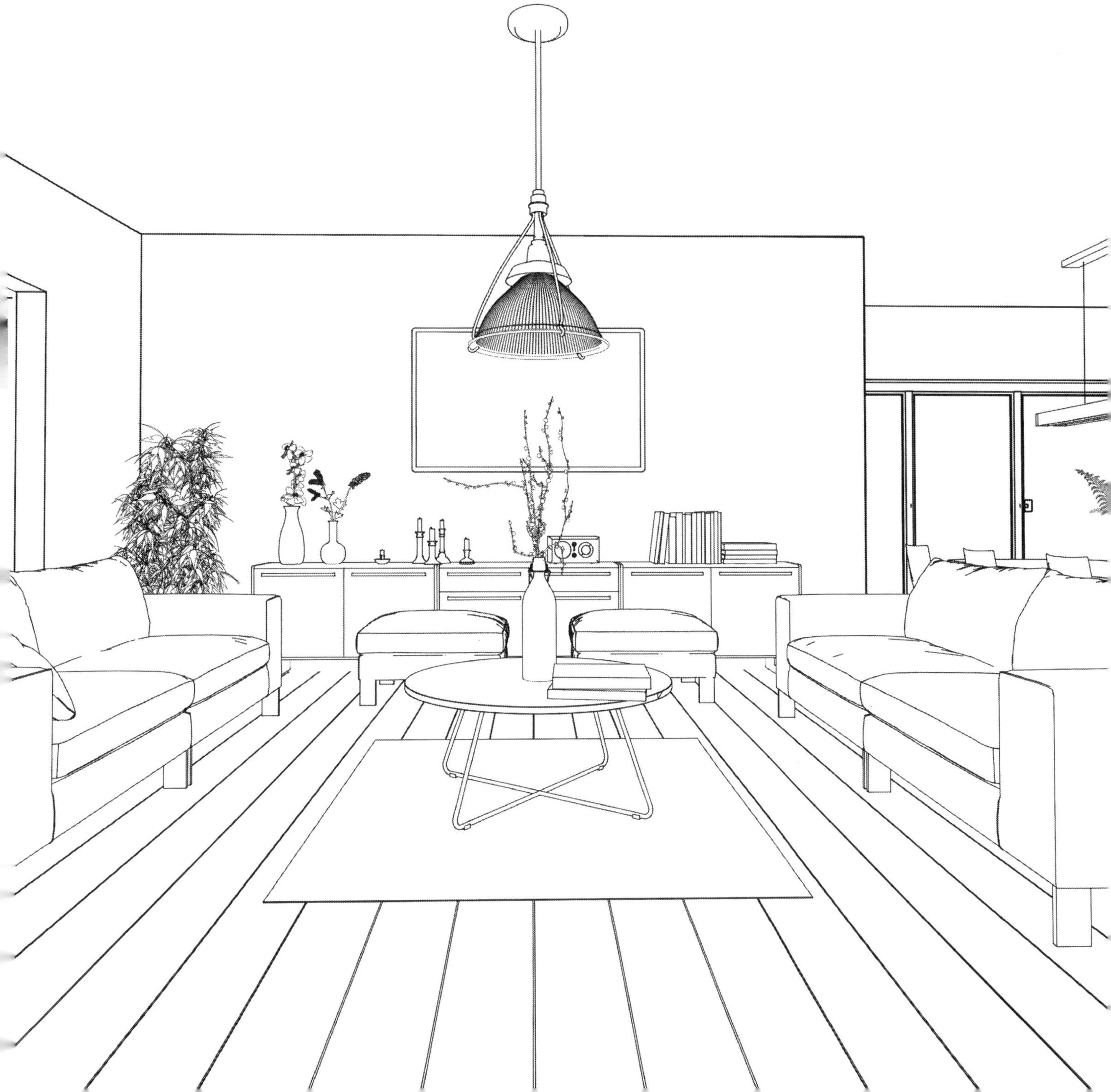

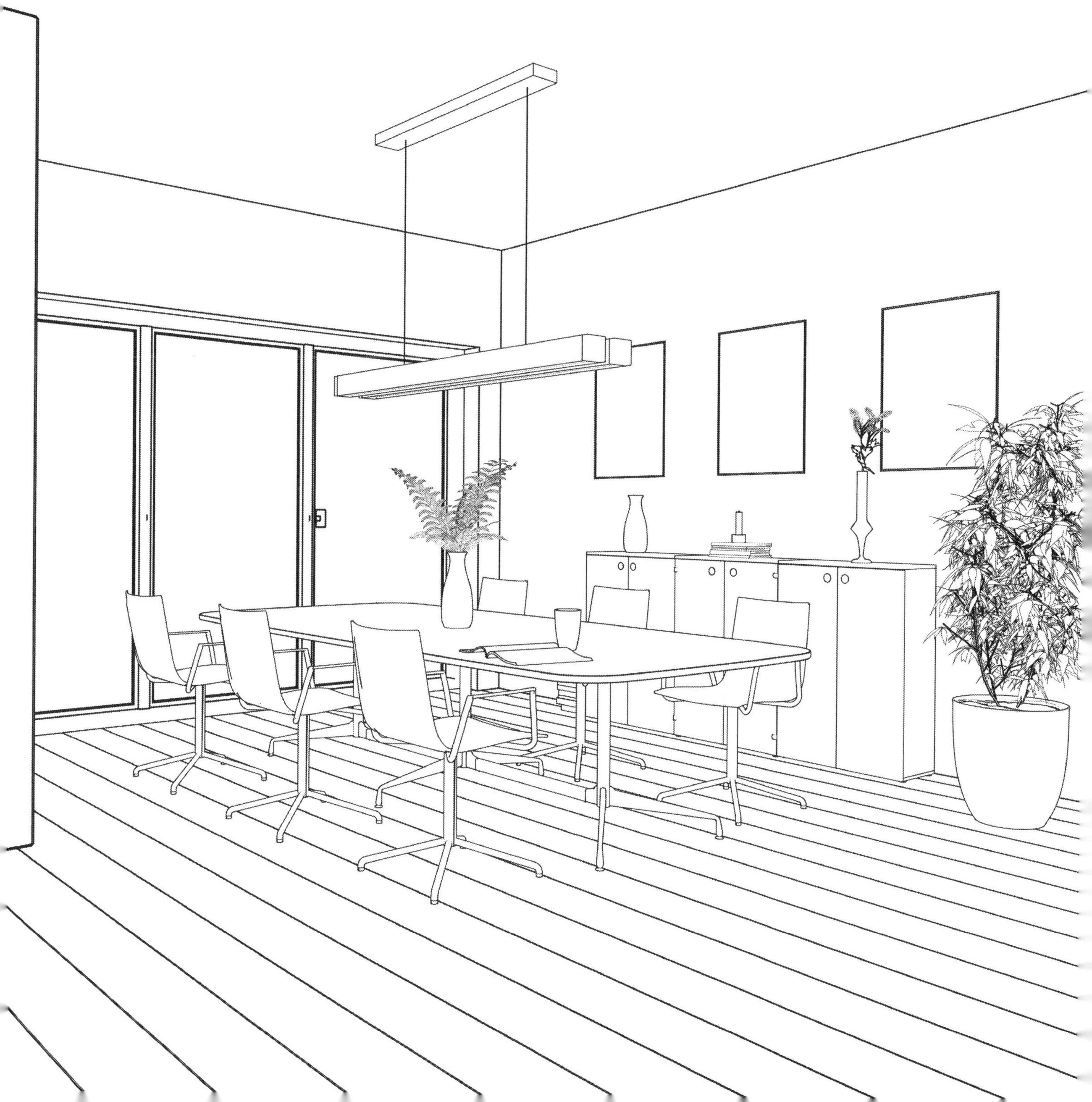

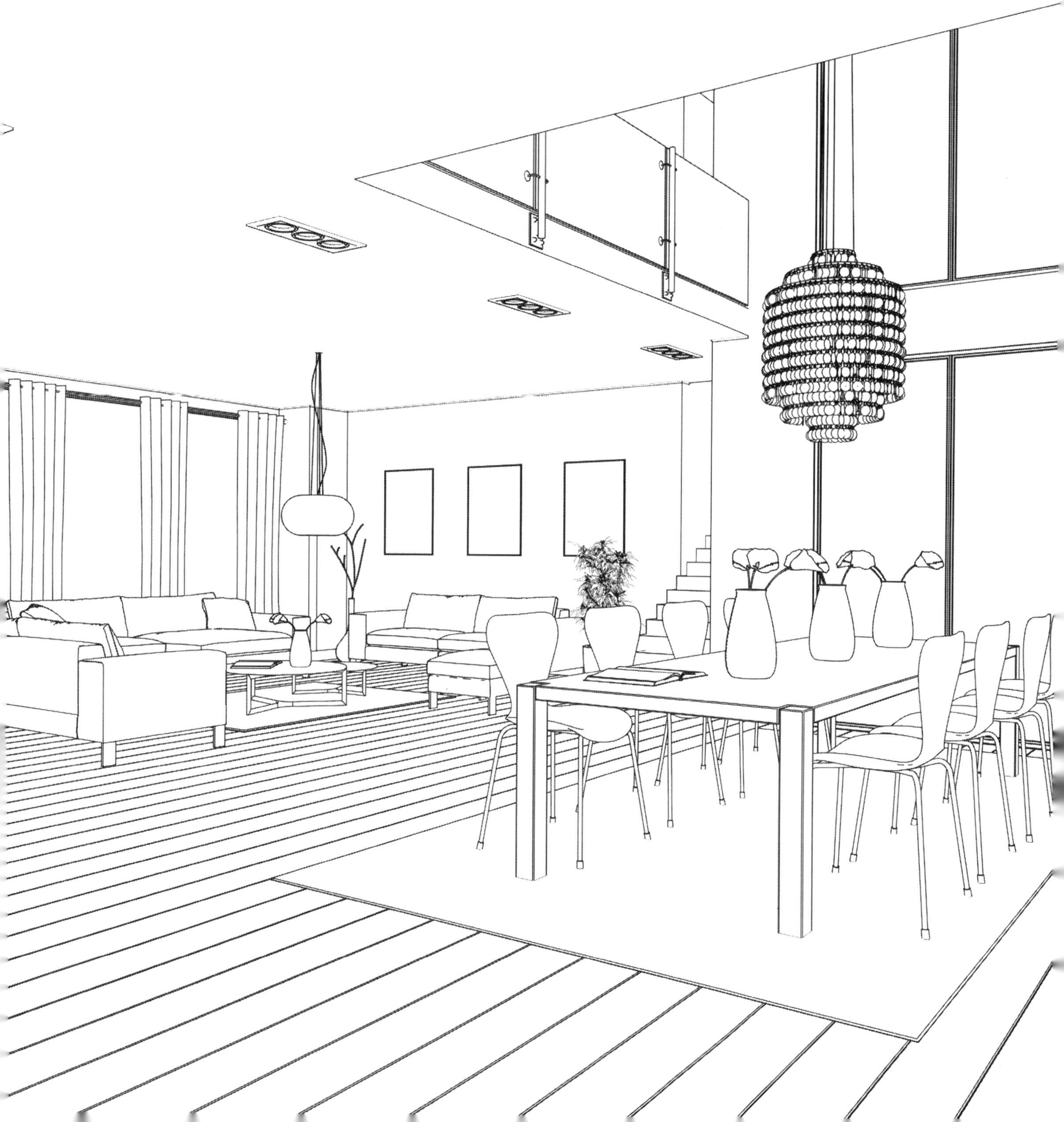

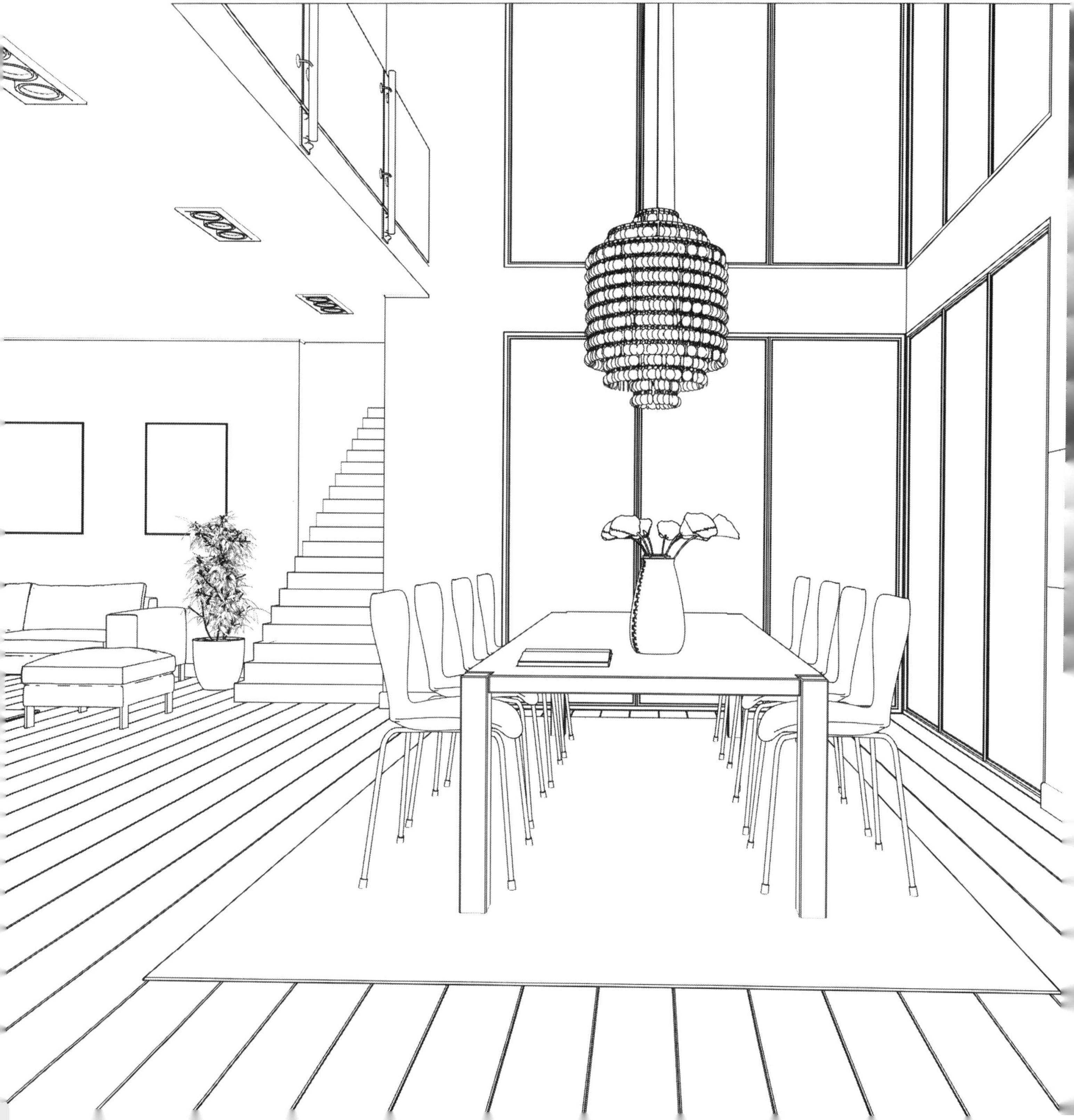

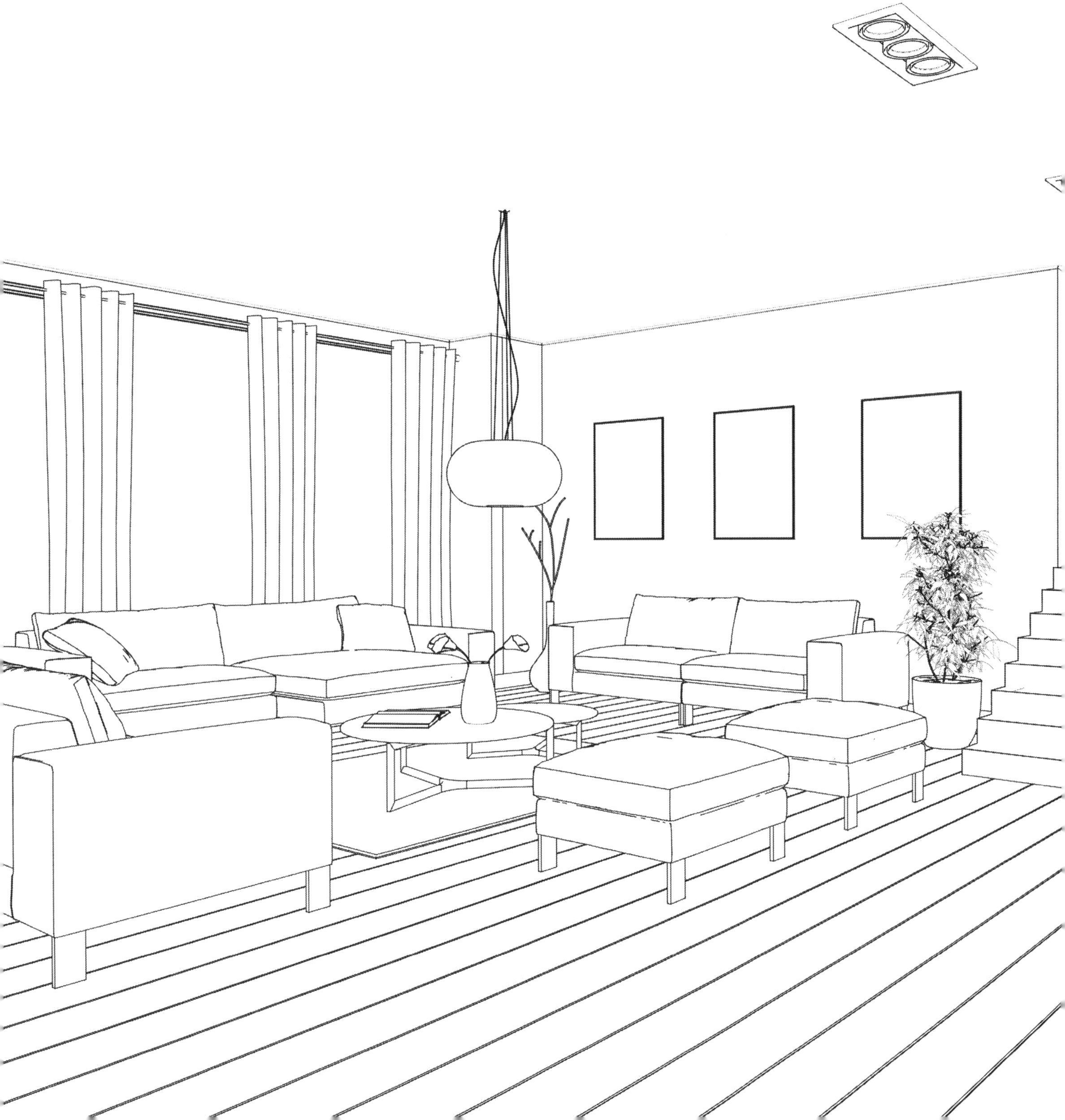

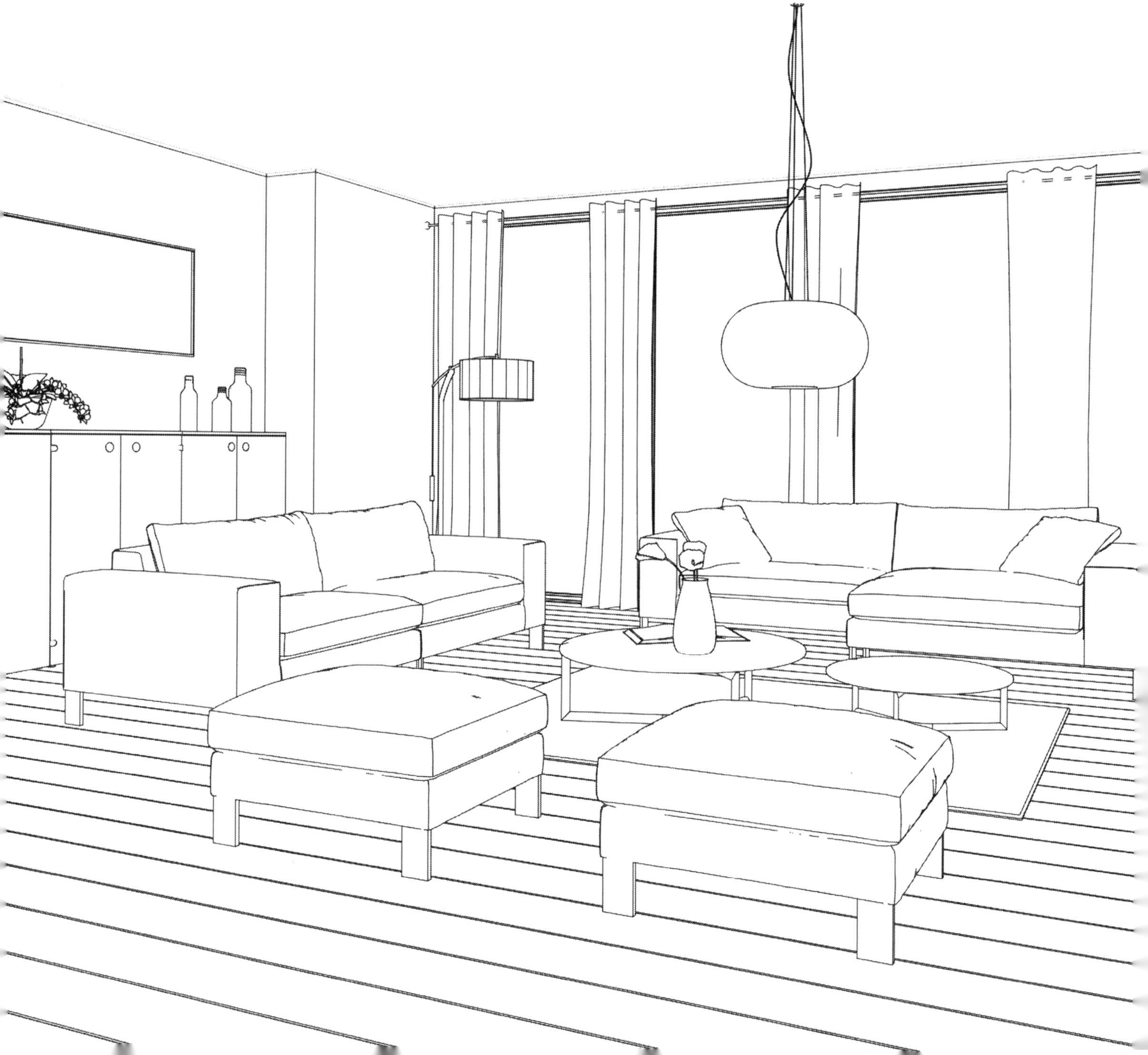

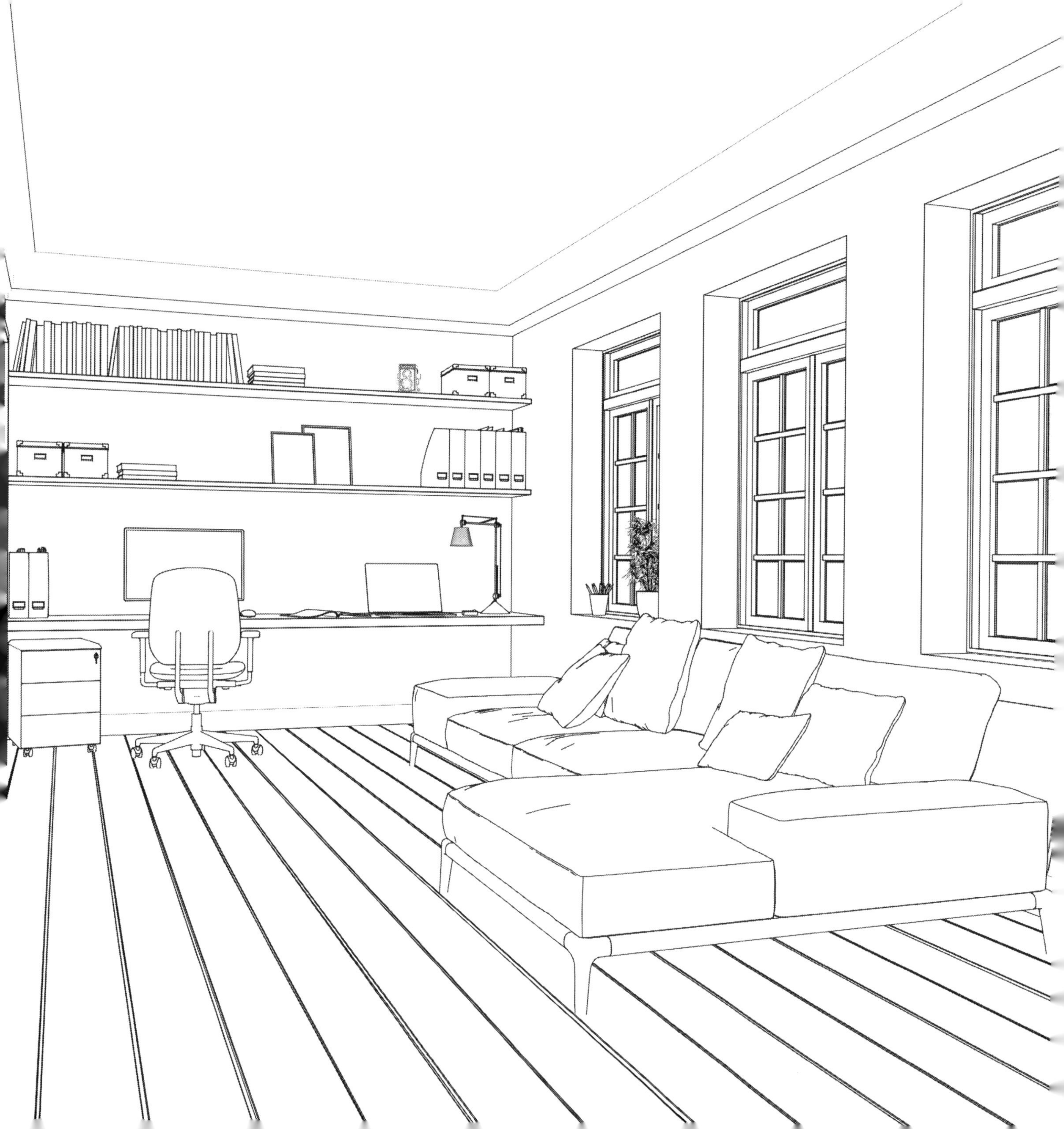

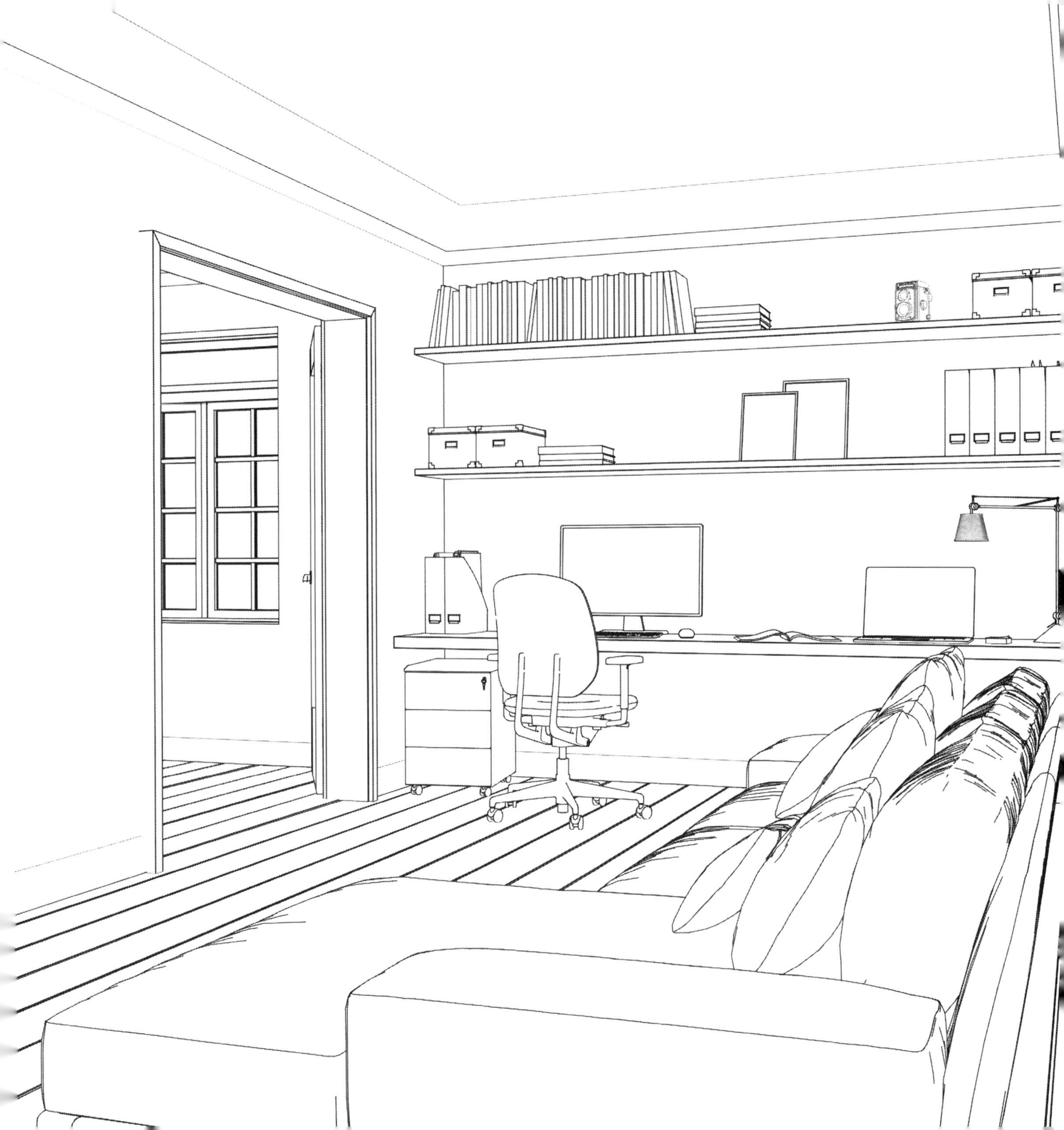

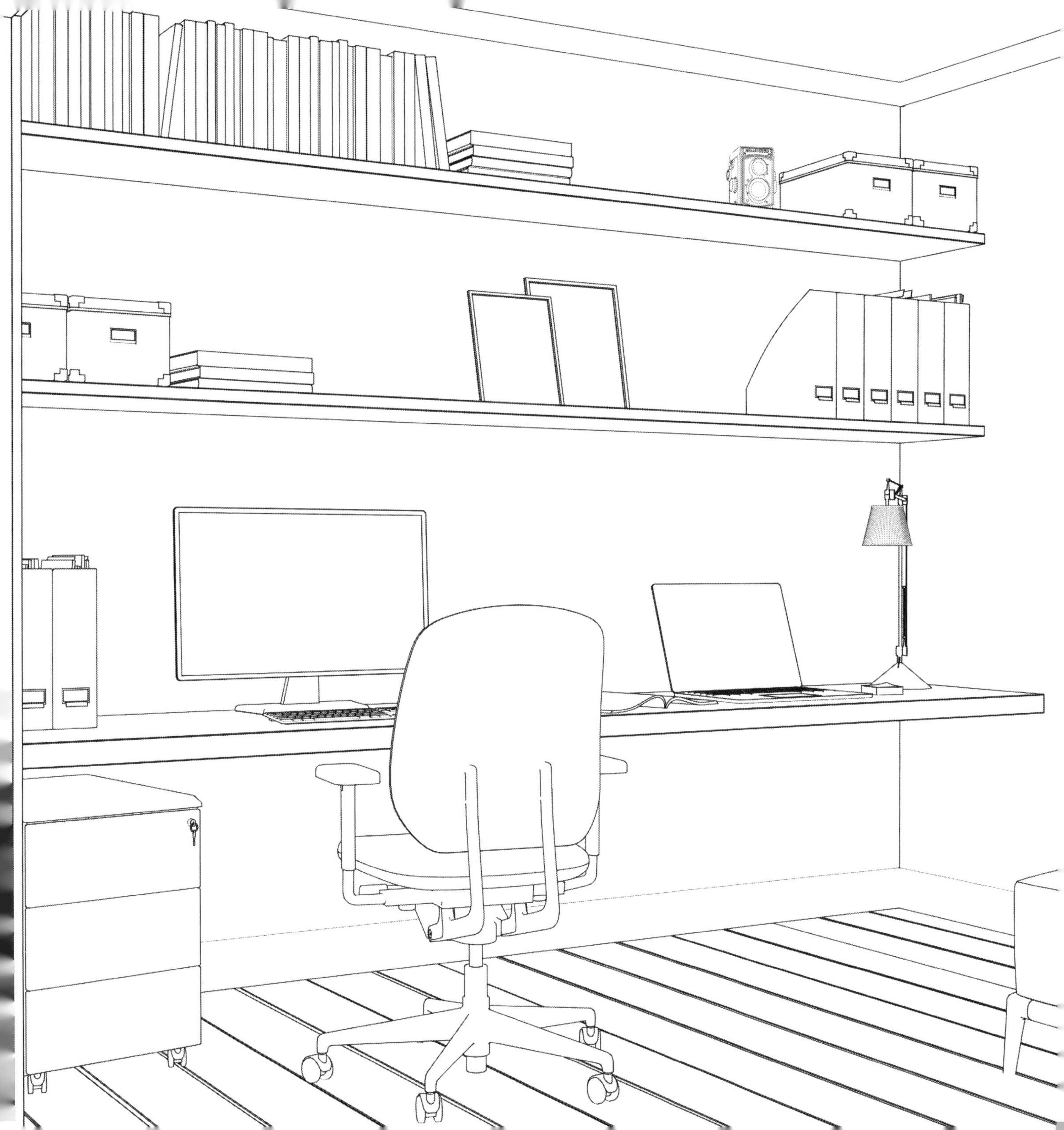

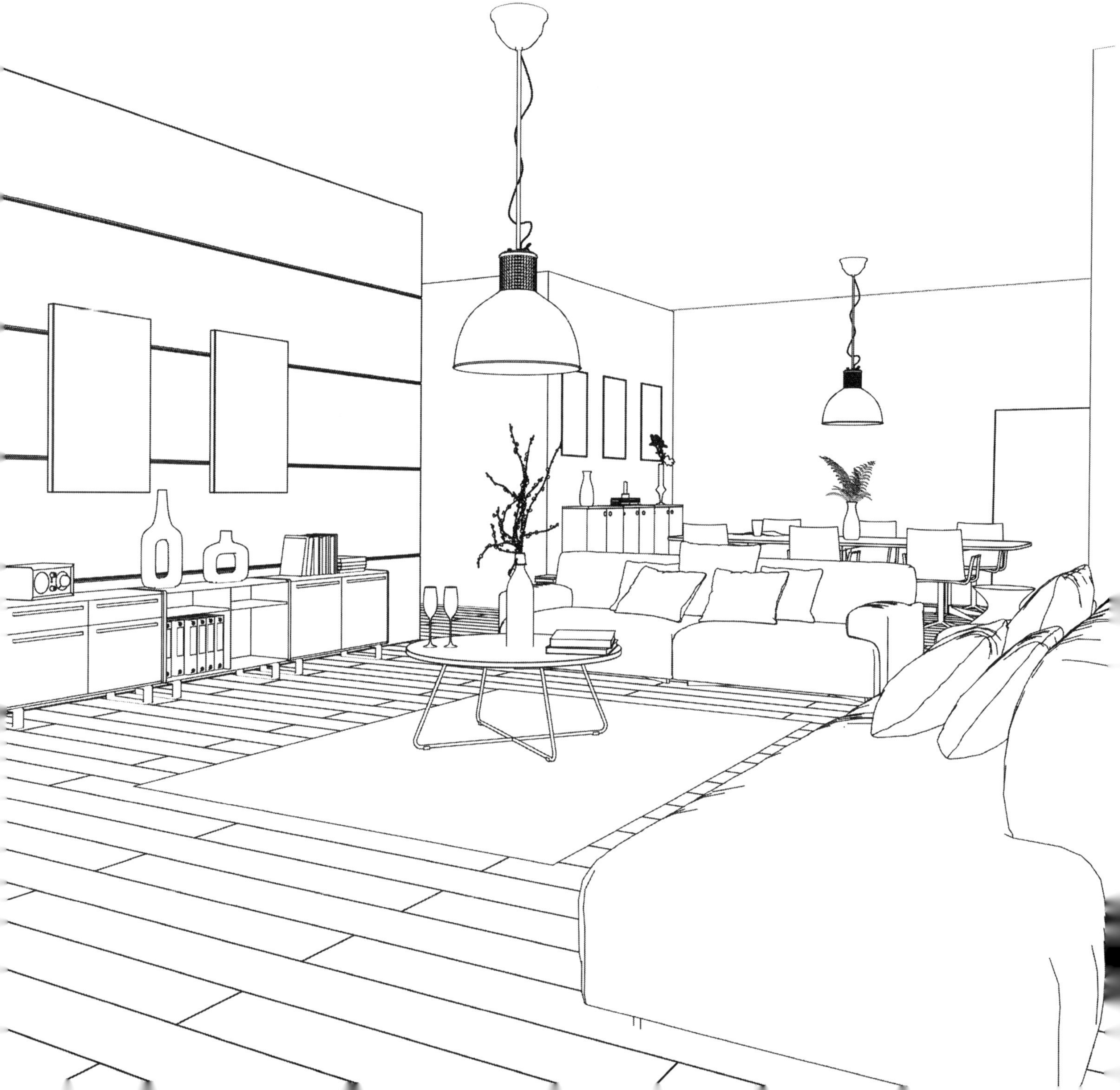

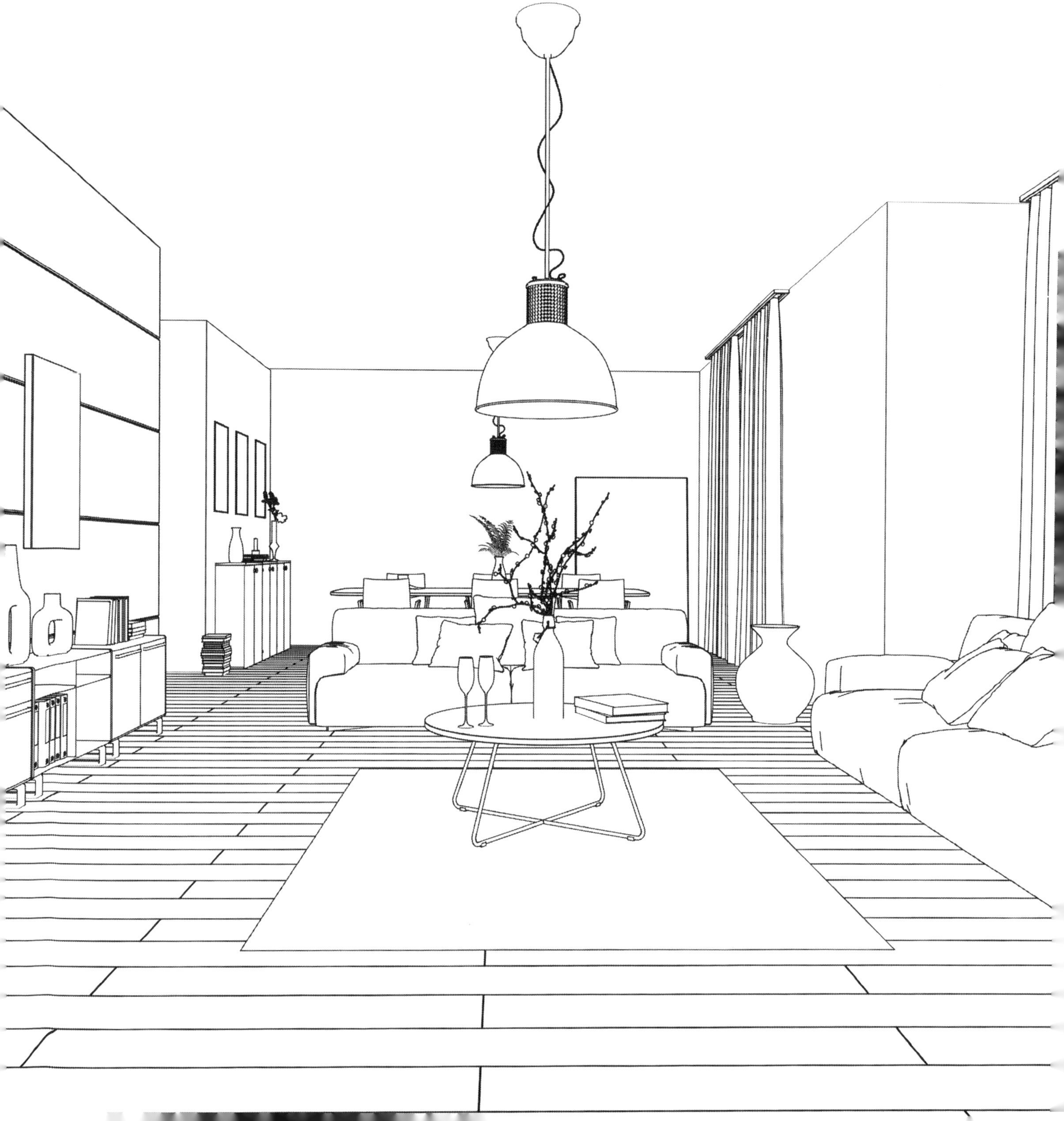

52800381R00046

Made in the USA
Lexington, KY
20 September 2019